All about
the St Bernard

Richard Beaver at
home with some of
the Lindenhall St
Bernards

All about the St Bernard

RICHARD and RACHEL BEAVER

PELHAM BOOKS

TO THE MEMORY OF
MRS R. L. WALKER
who knew and loved St Bernards for ninety years. The authors
will always be grateful for her help and encouragement.

PELHAM BOOKS

Published by the Penguin Group
27 Wrights Lane, London W8 5TZ. England
Viking Penguin Inc., 40 West 23rd Street, New York, New York 10010, USA
Penguin Books Australia Ltd, Ringwood, Victoria, Australia
Penguin Books Canada Ltd, 2801 John Street, Markham, Ontario, Canada L3R 1B4
Penguin Books (NZ) Ltd, 182–190 Wairau Road, Auckland 10, New Zealand

Penguin Books Ltd, Registered Offices: Harmondsworth, Middlesex, England

First published 1980

Copyright © 1980 by Richard J. Beaver

Revised edition 1988

ISBN 0 7207 1197 5

Typeset by Granada Typesetting
Printed and bound in Great Britain by
Butler & Tanner Ltd, Frome and London

Contents

Illustrations

Photographs

Line drawings

Tables

Illustration Sources

Photographs appear by courtesy of C. M. Cooke & Sons 50 and 52; Thomas Fall 24, 25, 29, 49, 66; Frank Garwood 53; H. Goater 36; Marc Henri 43; Melbourne Herald 61; Our Dogs 73; Diane Pearce 42, 48, 51, 70, 77; Mrs Pitts 69, 80; Sunday Mirror 1; M. Wensley 7.

Line Drawings by Terri Lawlor.

Acknowledgements

We are indebted to all who have supplied information and photographs for inclusion in this book, especially to the following.

W. F. Barazetti for permission to quote freely from *The St Bernard Books*. The late Mrs R. L. Walker and Mrs J. F. Briggs for much help with research on the early history of the breed in this country.
The Kennel Club and Clifford Hubbard for kindly making their libraries available.
Mrs M. Winterbottom for secretarial help.
Photographs are by Thomas Fall, who has skillfuly re-photographed many of the early prints, and Diane Pearce, C. M. Cooke & Son, *Dog World*, *Our Dogs* and Marc Henrie. The photograph of 'Barry' was taken from an old engraving in the possession of Michael Wensley.
The illustrations from *The Illustrated London News* and *Chatterbox* were kindly made available by W. Barazetti.

Introduction

All my life I had wanted a St Bernard, but the only canine companion of my youth was a Fox Terrier. Shortly after the last war, I went to live at Northbourne, in Kent, where I kept and worked gun dogs, and it was here I met the late Mrs Graydon Bradley, who kept a large kennel of St Bernards at nearby Whitfield Hall. She introduced me to Mrs Harding of Sholden Grange, and it was the latter who gave me my first St Bernard. This was a bitch out of Boystown Carol, by a son of Ch. Cornagarth Just Right, and I began to win with her in the show ring. Such was my enthusiasm, that she was soon joined by a second bitch of the same breeding, who was known as Gershwin Melody, and with whom I eventually won two Challenge Certificates. These were the days when the ring was dominated by the great Cornagarth and Peldator kennels, and one was lucky to take home even a red card from a Championship show. Melody had one litter, and it is from one of her daughters, kindly lent me by a friend for breeding, that my present bitch line is descended.

Soon after our marriage, my wife and I began to breed St Bernards seriously under the joint prefix Lindenhall. My wife still remembers how, when she was a small child, she was always taken for a brisk walk on Sunday afternoons, and how this constitutional often took her in the direction of Cliffsend Hall, at Pegwell Bay, where the late Mrs Sceales had her kennels. Notices outside the entrance warned that St Bernard dogs were loose in the grounds, and often a group of the massive creatures would be waiting behind the iron gates, ready to make friends with all who passed.

We had not been married long when we were asked if we would be prepared to give a home to an elderly St Bernard bitch. This proved to be none other than Sally, the last of Mrs Sceales's dogs, who had to leave the Hall when her mistress died. Sally settled down with us very happily, but when we moved from Kent to Derbyshire, she seemed to sense another disruption in her old life, and she never recovered from the move but died peacefully in her sleep shortly afterwards. She was twelve years old, and a dog we shall always remember with affection.

Shortly before we left Kent, the late Mr A. L. Gaunt asked me to look at a litter of St Bernard puppies for him in the Maidstone area. When my wife and I arrived at the house, we noticed that the front door had been boarded up. After we had seen the puppies, which were a fine litter, we were most surprised when the owner asked if we would care to have their mother. Apparently 'Treena' had just walked through the glass front door without opening it – for the third time! We thus acquired Cornagarth Adelaide, and never made a better buy; she was eventually mated to Mr Gaunt's German stud dog, Cornagarth Kuno Von Birkenkopf, and her resultant litter of seven puppies contained five Champions.

Since those early days we have had our share of bad luck as well as good; we have owned some wonderful dogs, and made a host of friends. I always think, however, that one remembers one's first dogs with the greatest nostalgia.

Often, when families visit our home in search of a St Bernard puppy, they say it has always been their ambition to own a member of this romantic and beautiful breed. In these circumstances I always attempt to point out the disadvantages and responsibilities that ownership entails. It is patiently explained that beauty and benevolence are accompanied by phenomenal strength, and voracious appetite, and that the costs involved are proportional to the size of the dog. I treat my visitors to lurid descriptions of huge muddy footprints on carpets, piles of moulted hair, slavering jaws, mounds of offal, and sonorous snores pervading the house throughout the night. If my warnings succeed in preventing the placing of a puppy in a home where he will eventually be unwelcome, I feel my time has been well spent.

I remember once being asked, on the telephone, to supply a St Bernard puppy to a woman living near London, and, as I had a feeling that all might not be well, I offered to take the puppy down to her. On arrival I was met by a little, old, partially-crippled lady, living in an immaculate small house, with a tiny garden, complete with goldfish pool, and plastic gnomes. She said she had seen a St Bernard on television, and thought she would like one! Fortunately, I was able to make her understand that a St Bernard was not the breed for her, and was able to fix her up with a dog of a smaller type. I feel sure a St Bernard would have had a wonderful time in that garden!

If, after my warnings, prospective owners are still convinced that they can cope with a St Bernard, it can be revealed that, although the romantic history of the life-saver of the Alps, complete with brandy flask, is now out of date, the St Bernard, if properly reared and trained, is indeed the King among Dogs as his honoured role as the emblem of the great Cruft's Show implies. He has all the good qualities one looks for in a dog, being faithful, loving, intelligent and gentle: he will make numerous friends wherever he takes his owner.

The new St Bernard owner becomes, as it were, a member of a race apart, and his living habits are gently but inexorably changed. A larger car, frequently of the estate type, appears in his driveway; low tables vanish from the living room, bolts are placed on previously easily-opened doors, and his garden, if small, ceases to be a place of beauty and becomes a mud-patch. Strange carvings and models of St Bernards appear on his mantleshelf, and brandy barrels, which have never held a drop of the hard stuff, are seen strangely suspended from the walls.

Always anxious to do his best for his puppy, round whom the household routine will henceforth revolve, the new owner seeks a book about the St Bernard breed. At the end of the last century, Hugh Dalziel produced one of the first books on the breed, and fifty years later we had W. F. Barazetti's excellent private publication, but unfortunately neither of these is now generally available. One or two American works are on sale in this country, but these deal exclusively with the St Bernards of the U.S.A. It is to fill this gap, and bring together what we hope may be useful and interesting information for all lovers of this wonderful breed, that my wife and I offer this book. We are most grateful to all who have been kind enough to supply information and photographs for inclusion, especially to Mr Barazetti for permission to quote freely from his earlier text. If in a small way our book does anything to further the interest of the St Bernard breed, the effort and enjoyment of writing it will have been well worthwhile.

Foreward to the Revised Edition

Since I wrote the above, eight years ago, the dog scene in Britain has greatly changed. More shows are offering Challenge Certificates to St Bernards, and new exhibitors are constantly appearing, to swell entries. There is now a shortage of experienced judges, because falling support for the smaller Open Shows has removed opportunities for gaining essential practical experience. Unless this tendency is checked it must inevitably lead to a lowering of standards.

In our increasingly affluent society, more large dogs are being purchased as status symbols and guard animals. The number of unwanted St Bernards constantly increases ... last year no less than fifteen were taken to Battersea Dogs' Home. Lack of conscience by a small section of breeders about the fate of the numerous puppies they produce is causing this problem for the 'Rescue' services, and it is disgraceful that commercial considerations should in some cases outweigh the welfare of the dogs concerned.

In 1986 the Kennel Club formulated a new standard for St Bernards, which unfortunately gives little guidance about the finer points of the breed. The International and American standards are printed in this book, and readers will find these much more helpfully descriptive about the points of the breed.

The problem in preparing this revised edition has been one of selection. Some material from the earlier text has had to be omitted to make room for updated items. We have been reluctant to discard historically interesting material, and have tried to strike a balance between the old and the new.

Tibetan Mastiffs.

1 The Origins of the St Bernard

Most of us became aware of the existence of the St Bernard in our childhood. We learned how this great dog had been bred for centuries in Switzerland by the monks of the lonely St Bernard Hospice, and how countless travellers, lost in the snowy wilderness of the mountains, owed their lives to its sagacity and strength. Little, however, was generally known of how this unique breed evolved, or from whence it came.

There were dogs in Switzerland in Neolithic times, but it is extremely unlikely that these were the forebears of the St Bernard. These early dogs were domesticated by the primitive inhabitants of the Swiss lake-side settlements, who lived in crude huts built on piles sunk in the margins of the lakes. Known as Marsh, or Turf Dogs, these animals were used for deer-hunting, and were light, agile creatures, quite unlike the St Bernard. All the members of the Mastiff group, to which the St Bernard belongs, are of heavy weight and bone, with large square heads, well-defined stops, and short, square muzzles; no traces of dogs of this type have yet been found among the prehistoric remains of Europe. We must therefore look further afield for the ancestors of the St Bernard, and our search ultimately takes us to Central Asia, to the foothills of the Himalayas, and to Ancient Tibet, where, in a breed known as the Tibetan Mastiff, lies the most probable clue to the origin of the St Bernard.

Because the Tibetan Mastiff has been used for centuries as a monastery guard, and regarded as a holy breed, it has survived unchanged over the years, and remains today as a living relic of the past. Like all mountain dogs, it is of tremendous size and weight, with a strong head, heavily-boned legs, and five-toed feet. It is said to be very savage, with a bark like the roar of a lion. It is still used today to guard the flocks of wandering tribesmen, and to protect women and children.

One of the earliest recorded mentions of a Tibetan Mastiff comes from China, dated A. D.1121, when the people of Liu, in the west of the country, sent one as a present to Won-Wang. This dog, which was known as Ngao, was said to measure 4 ft, and had been trained to hunt men of different colours. Later, in the Middle Ages, Marco Polo wrote: 'The people of Tibet possess a large number of powerful and excellent dogs, which render great service at the capture of musk deer. They keep dogs as big as donkeys, which are excellent for hunting wild animals, especially yak.'

According to ancient writers, these large dogs of Tibet, often erroneously known as 'Indian Dogs', were acquired by other races, and eventually introduced to Assyria and Babylon. Assyrian bas reliefs, in the British Museum, dated approximately 650 B. C., show dogs on hunting scenes which strongly resemble the modern St Bernard. The Assyrians used them as war dogs, and introduced them to Egypt. In 470 B.C., Xerxes, King of Persia, is believed to have taken some to Greece, but it was Alexander the Great who finally established them in Europe. On his march to the Indus, he is said to have received many presents of enormous dogs trained to do battle with lions and elephants. In 326 B.C. he was given 156 of these dogs, and used them in amphitheatres to fight against wild animals and gladiators. His tutor, Aristotle, gave them the name 'Leontonix', meaning 'sons of lions', as it was believed that these dogs had originally arisen from a cross between a dog and a lion. Though this would seem biologically impossible, St Bernards do often resemble great cats in attitude and expression.

One of Alexander's heirs, Pyrrhus, King of Epirus, temporarily conquered Italy, and so the dogs were introduced to the Romans. They called them 'Canis Molossus', after the town of Molossis in Epirus, where they believed they had originated. The dogs battled in the arenas of Rome, and were used for guard and herding duties. Columellus, who lived during the reign of Augustus, wrote of the Molossus: 'They are heavy of body, and have a sonorous bark that frightens all thieves; their colour is dark, they are thick-set, neither long nor short, and have a very big head, that looks the most important part of the animal; eyes black or greenish, wide chest, and well-covered with hair, broad-shouldered, legs thick, and nails large.'

The Roman Molossus developed into two distinct types. One, of slight build and light colour, with a long head, was used as a herding dog. The other, heavier and more massive, was dark-coated, and had a broad head. It was used for guard duties, and as a fighting dog, and from this heavier type of Molossus the St Bernard and the Mastiff have almost certainly descended. The name 'Mastiff' may well be a derivation of the Latin word 'massivus'.

Before Roman times, Molossus-type dogs had been brought from Asia to Britain by Phoenician sailors, and a separate strain developed in these islands. When the Romans conquered Britain, they took a number of the British Molossus home with them to Italy, but although these dogs were even larger than their own, both strains had developed from a common Asian ancestry.

As the Roman armies advanced northward into Europe over the Alps, their dogs accompanied them. In about 40 B. C., the Roman invaders into Switzerland travelled by the Mons Jovis, later the St Bernard Pass, where they built a temple to Jupiter. At this time the lighter type of herding Molossus was introduced into the Alpine valleys. It is today represented by the smaller type of Swiss herd dog, known as the Sennenhunde, of which there are several varieties, including the Appenzeller and the Bernese. The skull of a dog excavated at the Roman settlement of Vindonissa in Switzerland is typical of the Swiss Sennenhunde of today.

During later Roman invasions, in the first and second centuries A. D., the heavier type of Molossus reached Switzerland. These dogs remained as guards in the passes, and in the Aosta and Valais districts, the eventual home of the St Bernard. Later, these Mastiff-type dogs reached Berne and the Jura, and were used not only as guards but also as working farm dogs. They are believed to have developed into the larger breeds of herd dog, and into the St Bernard.

Throughout the centuries, the Valais district remained geographically isolated because of the few routes of communication with other areas. A pure strain of dogs therefore developed there, as only occasionally could any foreign blood be introduced. When the monks of the Great St Bernard Hospice began, during the seventeenth century, to use dogs to assist in Alpine rescue, it was from this pure Valais strain that they selected their original stock. There are many records of later occasions when the numbers of dogs at the Hospice were reduced to negligible numbers, and the monks must have constantly replenished their strain from outside sources in the district. The world-wide fame so worthily earned by the rescue dogs at the Hospice led eventually to the breed name 'St Bernard', but one should remember that this unique type of dog developed initially not only at the Hospice but in the whole Valais district.

2 The Hospice and its Dogs

The Hospice of the Great St Bernard stands at over 8,000 ft above sea level at the top of the Great St Bernard Pass in the Swiss Canton of Valais. It is one of the highest human habitations in Europe. Lacking the beauty of many other mountain passes, the Great St Bernard is a place of bleak snow-covered rocks and jagged peaks which tower over the small Hospice buildings huddled below them. On the Plan de Jupiter, a small plateau formerly occupied by the Mons Jovis temple, stands the iron statue of St Bernard pointing the way to his Hospice. 'You who climb the Alps in safety under my guidance', says the plaque below, 'continue with me into the House of Heaven.'

The climate in the Pass is such that little vegetation can grow, and a few pine trees about 2,000 ft below are the only signs of life on the treacherous slopes. For only about twenty days annually is the area free from snow, ice and frost. The small lake in front of the Hospice buildings, which forms part of the boundary between Italy and Switzerland, is sometimes frozen throughout the year. During the winter months, the snow has reached a depth of 36 ft around the buildings, and it is possible to ski right out of the windows on the second storey.

This Pass, on the main road between Italy and Northern Europe, has always been one of the most important routes across the Alps. The Romans improved it during the first century A. D., and it was much used by Christian pilgrims journeying to the Tomb of the Apostles in Rome. These people were often the victims of gangs of Saracen robbers who lay in wait for those using the Pass, and used as their main hide-out the ruined Temple of Jupiter, built by the Romans.

Bernard de Menthon was born in Savoy at the end of the tenth century A. D. He was the son of Richard de Menthon, a wealthy baron who resided at the Castle of Menthon on the Lake of Annecy, which is still in the possession of his descendants to this day. Bernard is known to have studied theology in Paris until his proud parents demanded his return to Menthon to marry a rich heiress. Bernard, who was determined to become a monk, tore the bars from his window on the night before the wedding, and escaped. He fled to the Augustinian Cathedral at Aosta in Italy, where he later became a canon, and eventually Archdeacon.

The Statue of St Bernard de Menthon, on the Plan de Jupiter.

Facing Page The Hospice of the Great St Bernard.

According to legend, frightened villagers burst in one night as Bernard was praying in his chapel, claiming to have been attacked by the devil Procus who was said to worship at the temple of Jupiter. Bernard led the villagers up through a terrible storm to the temple. Procus turned himself into a dragon, but Bernard threw his stole around the devil's neck, and it turned into a chain, which held him down while Bernard slew him. The villagers demolished the statue of Jupiter, and Bernard told them to build a Hospice in the pass for the shelter and protection of travellers. This they did in about 962 A. D., dragging some of the stone for many miles over icy tracks, and constructing a simple building like one of the refuge huts frequently found in the mountains. Bernard's parents, who had been grief-stricken since his departure, visited him there, and donated much of their wealth towards the completion and maintenance of his Hospice. Bernard died at the age of 85, having served as an Archdeacon for 40 years.

It is impossible to say with certainty when dogs were first introduced to the Hospice, as all its early archives were destroyed in a disastrous fire in 1555. A picture of St Bernard which hangs in the Hospice today shows him with a dog, but this was probably painted in the nineteenth century. Another picture, painted about 1695 by a Neapolitan artist, shows two dogs of St Bernard type. In 1707 we have the first written mention, in the writings of a monk, who states, 'a dog was buried by snow this day'. In the following year there is mention of a Canon Vincent Cosmos 'making a wheel in which a dog is placed to turn the spit'. With hundreds of hungry travellers to be fed at all hours of the day and night, meat was almost constantly roasting on a revolving spit, and the monks must have found dogs very useful for this purpose, but if St Bernards were used for this task, the spit wheels must have been of great size.

It seems probable that dogs were first brought to the Hospice between 1660 and 1670. They would have been obtained from the valleys, and have been of the distinctive Valais type which had developed from the old Roman Molossus. No doubt it was soon discovered that their sense of smell and direction were of help in finding people lost in snow and fog, and so a partnership between dogs and monks would have been gradually built up. In the harsh mountain conditions, dogs of great stamina and size with short, thick, weather-resistant coats and marked intelligence would have been necessary. Almost certainly, a strain showing these qualities was gradually built up by selective breeding. As this distinctive strain developed, it became known as the Hospice dog. Much crossing must always have taken place with dogs from the valleys and from those belonging to associated Hospices at the Simplon and Little St Bernard Passes.

The qualities of St Bernards which make them so invaluable for Alpine rescue work are well known. Not only can they scent a human being against the wind up to two miles away, but they can locate a body buried by as much as ten feet of snow. They have a wonderful presentiment which enables them to sense a dangerous blizzard about twenty minutes before it occurs. They have been known to give warning of avalanches, standing still and changing course before the dreaded falls take place. All these qualities, coupled with their great strength, gentleness, and ability to work for hours in sub-zero temperatures, have made possible their amazing record of success in Alpine rescue work.

Until about 1830 it is believed that all the Hospice dogs were smooth-coated. From time to time the numbers were depleted by illness or by the hazards of snow and avalanche, and when this happened new blood was introduced from the valleys to revive the strain. Crossing no doubt took place with the Sennenhunde and other

St Bernard type dog from a picture at the Hospice painted about 1695.

A Canon of the Great St Bernard Hospice exercises two of his dogs.

mountain breeds, but when this occurred the change in appearance would be only temporary as it would soon be largely eliminated by crossing back to the original Hospice strain. Soon after the Napoleonic wars, a Newfoundland cross was used, as it was believed the thicker coats would give increased protection from the cold. It soon proved that longer coated specimens were useless for Alpine conditions, as ice balls formed in the coats, eventually encasing the dogs in frozen strait-jackets. For this reason, any rough-coated puppies born were sold or given away to benefactors, so a distinct type of rough-coated Hospice dog became fairly common in the valleys near the monastery.

The monks' ideal St Bernard had a white blaze running right up the face from nose to neck, and a white collar encircling the neck and traversing the shoulders and chest. The orange colour on the head deepened towards the white until it became black at the fringe. In the centre of the white, on the forehead, a dark spot was thought to be desirable. These markings were said to represent the stole, chasuble and scapular which formed part of the vestments worn by the monks.

The most famous of the Hospice dogs was Barry, who worked there from 1800 to 1812, and its reputed to have saved at least forty lives. At the earliest sign of fog or snow, Barry would become restless and demand to be let out. Once outside, he would begin searching in the most remote and dangerous places. Whenever he was unable to dig a person out of the snow himself, he would run back to the Hospice to fetch the assistance of the monks. One of his most famous exploits was the rescue of a small boy, the victim of an avalanche, who was stranded on a snow-covered ledge. Having located the child, Barry covered him with his body to warm him, and licked his face to revive him. The child was then able to climb on his back, and was carried to the safety of the Hospice. The exhausted dog then led a party of monks to the body of the child's mother, who was lying dead in the snow as if asleep. There is a story that Barry found a soldier lying in the snow, and that the man, frozen and confused, mistook the dog for a wolf and killed him with his sword. It is more likely, however, that Barry grew too old for work, and the Prior sent him to end his days in retirement with friends at Berne, where he died some two years later. His stuffed body can still be seen there in the Natural History Museum, and, to this day, one of the dogs at the Hospice has always born the name 'Barry', after his famous predecessor.

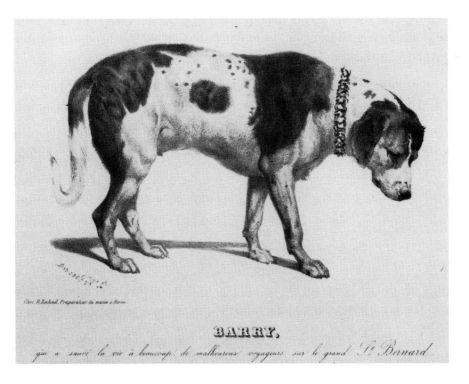

BARRY,

qui a sauvé la vie à beaucoup de malheureux voyageurs sur le grand S.t Bernard

The famous Hospice dog Barry (1800-1814). This picture, taken from an engraving in the possession of Michael Wensley, shows Barry as he stood in the Natural History Museum at Berne, before the body was re-set in a different position in 1923.

A dramatic tale of a robbery attempt at the Hospice is told by W. F. Barazetti. It appears that one night in October 1787 the monks gave hospitality to two men who arrived at the monastery from Italy. They posed as silversmiths, and showed professional interest in the treasures of the Order. The Prior proudly showed them all the valuables, including the tenth-century jewelled crucifix, the heavy golden chalice presented in 1507, and the magnificent collection of Roman coins. Next morning two strangers left, but, instead of proceeding to Switzerland, they retraced their steps to Italy, to report what they had seen to the rest of their gang, and to complete arrangements for a robbery. They had no fear of the dogs, for they planned to take with them a bitch in season, to act as a distraction.

Several days later, when the Pass was blanketed in thick, dangerous, fog, all the dogs left the Hospice, with most of the monks, to search for lost travellers. Suddenly, one of the dogs stopped dead in his tracks, and sniffed the air in the direction of the Hospice. Slowly it moved again in a strange, uneasy manner, crouching and growling. Then all the pack made off, rushing madly towards home over the snow-covered rocks, with the monks running vainly behind them. The monks stumbled and fell, and soon there was no sign of the dogs in the enveloping fog. When the monks eventually reached the Hospice, they found the great door battered open, and a scene of silent confusion within. At last the Prior appeared with his robes torn. He told how, soon after he had gone to bed, the Italian gang had arrived and had smashed their way into the building. When he had confronted them, he had been forced at pistol point to the chapel, and made to unlock the strongroom containing the treasures. With the two 'silversmiths' guiding them, the gang had loaded the valuables into a leather sack. Just as they had finished their work, the bitch they had brought with them growled, screamed and fled. There were the Hospice dogs! One made straight for the man with the sack, which fell, spilling its contents on the ground. A knife flashed, and the dog collapsed, with blood spilling over golden coins. In the resultant chaos, the robbers rushed off into the darkness and the fog, followed by the enraged pack of dogs. Then there was silence. At midnight, the dogs returned alone, many wounded; of the gang who had tried to rob the Hospice, nothing was ever seen again.

The story is told of another band of robbers who also posed as pilgrims. Having eaten well, they demanded that the Prior should take them to the place where the valuables were kept. This Prior, however, was less gullible. He took them to the dogs instead. They left at once, quietly!

Throughout the centuries the Hospice has provided shelter for rich and poor alike, and many famous people have crossed its threshold.

When Napoleon travelled the Pass in the spring of 1800 on his way to his great victory against the Austrians at Marengo, he was accompanied by an army of 40.000 men. Each of his 58 cannon was encased in a hollowed-out tree trunk, to be dragged up the mountains by a team of 40 grenadiers. When they reached the Hospice, all the soldiers were given hospitality. One of the officers, Captain Coiget, wrote:

'After fantastic exertions we reached the Hospice. We left the guns and entered, altogether 400 grenadiers and a handful of officers. The monks have dedicated a lifetime to the welfare of humanity, helping and refreshing all travellers. The dogs are always at hand to guide those unlucky ones who lose their way, and lead them back to the house where they find help and charity. While our officers and the colonel sat in the hall by the fire, the venerable clergymen gave each twelve men a bucketful of wine, a quarter of cheese, and a pound of bread, and showed us where to rest in those wide passages. These good men really did everything they could, and I think they were also treated well themselves. We shook hands with the good padres when we left, and we stroked their dogs, who came to us as if they had known us for a long time. I find it difficult to express in words the respect and admiration I feel for these men.'

Napoleon's general, Chambarlhac, who was in charge of the expedition, had to watch helplessly as one gun fell down a precipice, taking ten soldiers with it before they could free their frozen hands from the ropes. When he reached the Hospice, he found he had lost a hundred men. Soon, Napoleon himself arrived, and was received by the Prior, Louis Antoine Luger, and two monks.

'Are you three up here on your own all winter?', he asked.

'No, we are about twenty altogether, with our dogs to help us rescue the lost.'

'And where are your men and your dogs, while my soldiers perish, may I ask?'

'They are out to rescue them, sire!'

And so they were! The ten soldiers that went over the precipice had given up all hope of rescue, and, icy and numb, had begun to drowse in the snow, awaiting a peaceful death. Suddenly, the bark of a dog roused one, who managed to stir two of his companions, and together they stumbled in the direction of the sound. After a few moments, three St Bernards rushed through the snow and threw the soldiers down, licking them and making them see the brandy kegs round their necks. Soon two monks arrived to help, and all returned to arouse the other seven soldiers and free them from the snow. When the party arrived back at the Hospice, Napoleon was still there. He asked for a personal report, and was able to see the dogs. His young general,

Desaix, played with the dogs, and said they made him 'feel at home'. Only a fortnight later, Napoleon had won the victory which was to make him master of Europe for more than a decade, but his favourite, Desaix, lost his life in the battle. Remembering the happy episode at the Hospice, Napoleon ordered that his general's body should be taken there. 'Lay him in the home he chose;' said Napoleon, 'the dogs will guard him well!' So, today, the name of General Desaix can still be seen inscribed on a marble plate in the chapel at the Hospice, where his body lies.

Another famous visitor to the Hospice was Queen Victoria, who stayed there for one night and later presented the monks with her portrait. During the 1840s she had a dog and a bitch sent to her from Switzerland. Her son, Edward VII, visited the monastery when he was eighteen, and was presented with a St Bernard puppy, which unfortunately died during the journey home. As a mark of gratitude for the hospitality he had received, he sent the monks a piano, and many years later, after he became King, he sent another, to show the monks he had not forgotten them.

Not all visitors to the Hospice are human. Twice a year, in April and October, the monks open the Hospice windows to admit tens of thousands of swallows who enter the buildings to seek a night's shelter during their long migratory journey between Europe and Africa.

At one time, about twenty thousand people used to cross the Great St Bernard Pass each year. Many were Italian workmen who went north in the spring in search of work, and returned to Italy in the late autumn. The road constructed in 1890 was only passable during the summer months, and so narrow that up-going traffic was restricted to the morning hours, and downward traffic to the afternoons. Supplies of food, including horsemeat and meal for the dogs, were taken up by road in summer and stored for winter use.

Between 1888 and 1939, Theophilus Bourgeois remained as one of the longest-serving Provosts at the Hospice, and during this time did much to improve the conditions there. He was responsible for the installation of telephone, electricity, and central heating, and he also ordered the construction of the building now used as an hotel. With improvement in communications and the tunnelling of the Great St Bernard in 1964, the need for a rescue service has greatly declined. Travellers who cross the pass on foot during the dangerous season are now extremely rare, as other means of communication are much quicker and safer, but the number of skiers grows each year. During the summer, when the road is open, coaches bring noisy crowds of tourists to visit the monastery, but the monks will now only provide accommodation for the needy and for members of youth organisations. Life for the friars, however, is still rigorous: most of them are young

No. 31. *June 12, 1891.*   *Weekly — One Halfpenny*

Chatterbox.

St. Bernard to the rescue

'St Bernard to the Rescue' reproduced from the cover of *Chatterbox* magazine, 1891.

men, and expert skiers, and an eight-year limit is put on the time they are permitted to remain at the Hospice, as the altitude affects even the strongest hearts.

A Hospice St
Bernard
of the 1950s.

During the period immediately following the World War II, the
Hospice St Bernard kennels were greatly re-organised. New, modern
buildings to house the dogs were constructed behind the hotel, and
competent kennel staff took charge. Affiliation to the Swiss St Bernard
Club took place, and official pedigrees were issued and breeding records
kept. The kennel became not only a tourist attraction, but a successful
commercial enterprise, and puppies bred there were sold to many
countries throughout the world. During winter, only a few dogs now
remain at the Hospice to work as mountain guides, and the majority are
sent to a farm in the valley, where they spend the winter in less severe
conditions.

In 1933 a group of monks from the Hospice set out for the barren
Latza Pass in Tibet to found a monastery similar to that in
Switzerland. They took a group of their dogs with them, and so the St
Bernard finally returned to the home of its ancient forebears.

3 The Advent of the Show Dog

The Hospice Monks created the St Bernard as a working dog capable of carrying out its duties under the most arduous conditions, and they had to be highly selective in their breeding programme. There was no place for any 'passengers' at the Hospice. Any dogs falling short of the monk's exacting requirements, perhaps because of lack of size or stamina, too much roughness of coat, or unsuitable temperaments, were disposed of to outsiders. Often the new owners used these dogs for breeding, so dogs of Hospice type became fairly common in the locality of the monastery. Haphazard crossing of these dogs, often with other breeds, resulted in great diversification of type, and any dog with a modicum of monastery blood in its veins was often sold by the unscrupulous as a 'Hospice Dog'.

By the middle of the nineteenth century, industrial progress had begun to bring more leisure and prosperity to certain sections of the community, and it began to be common practice to keep dogs not only for work but for pleasure also. Improvement in road and rail communications made travelling less difficult, and it began to be possible for breeders to go further afield for stud services, and to attend shows. In Britain, the first dog show, confined to Spaniels only, had been held at the Zoological Gardens, London, in 1843, and the sport soon gained in popularity. The first St Bernards were exhibited at Cremorne in 1863, and soon a craze for the breed began in this country, and many animals were imported from Switzerland. Many of the early imports were of indifferent type, and it was mainly from the stock imported from Heinrich Schumacher, of Hollingen, near Berne, that the foundations of the breed in Britain were laid.

Schumacher (1831–1903) was a man of unusual talent and determination, and made a life-time study of the St Bernard. He was the first enthusiast outside the Hospice to breed systematically for a desired type, and in 1867 he compiled the first Stud Register of the breed. He was said to know every dog of Hospice descent in Switzerland. His extensive writings included a detailed history of the breed, issued in a Swiss Kynological Society publication in 1884.

Schumacher's ideal St Bernard was of the old Barry type, which had been typical of the Hospice dogs before the introduction of the Newfoundland cross. He aimed for a smooth-coated dog of moderate size, 'and wanted his dogs to be active, intelligent, and able to move like 'horses not cattle'. He criticised other Swiss breeders for producing over-large animals, with enormous heads 'too round and thick, and short in the nose'. Schumacher's breeding stock was acquired from all over the country, including the Hospice, and he sold some of his dogs back to the monks to improve their own strain. When he brought one pair of dogs to the Hospice in 1866, tears are said to have filled the eyes of the Prior, who said of one of them: 'That is indeed old Barry of 1814 standing there!'

Schumacher gave an interesting account of the breed in Switzerland outside the Hospice, and of the foundations of his own kennel, in a paper published in 1886, some of which makes interesting reading:

'The dogs presented from the St Bernard Hospice, and their offspring, I have known mostly since 1838. All of these were red with white marks, black face, black neck, and double wolf claws, and of a height not since attained; strongly built, particularly deep-chested, and with large and noble heads.

The dogs in Mettlen were long-haired, with fine, high-worn feather tail; and their offspring, I have observed since the beginning of 1850, were always trained in the same way as the parents had been. Most of the long-haired so-called St Bernard dogs, or Bernardiner, are to be found in a degenerate state in Berne.

The dogs of Bussy, near Valengin, were short-haired, red, with white marks. Amongst them was the most beautiful and most powerful female I ever saw, which I knew from 1846 to 1849. I tried to get puppies from the owner, but unfortunately could not do so.

Colonel Risold of Berne, had only one dog (a male) from the end of 1830 to 1840 – short-haired, with the same markings and the same colour as the others of enormous head. It was so strong and courageous as to be the terror and master of all the other dogs in Berne. It has no known offspring. The dogs of Messrs Cornaz I did not recognise as being amongst the progenitors received from the Hospice. These were erect, long-haired, double-clawed, white with reddish brown heads. Several specimens are stump-tailed.

The dogs from Lowenberg I have known since 1838, for I passed a considerable time in Murten. In 1854, my Barry I was born in Lowenberg – short-haired, white, with red head. As he resembled neither in his hair, nor his colour, the preceding generation, the owners entertained the erroneous impression that he was a mongrel and did not think he was a rare example, a freak of Nature; and they sold him as valueless to Mr Klopfenstein, from whom I acquired the dog in 1855, principally because this was the only dog which possessed such a striking resemblance to Barry of 1815 in the Natural History Museum and because I knew his pedigree. From Barry I, I have bred magnificent pups which were mostly sold in Russia, until Mr Baron Judd, of Glockenthal, near Thun, bought Barry from me in 1858, on condition that pups should be given to me as soon as possible. He experienced difficulty in finding females of similar breed.

The Revd Mr Weyerman, of Interlachen, possessed Blass, a large, long-haired, very fine St Bernard female, resulting from the crossing of a Hospice dog, which female, by Barry I, produced Sultan I. Sultan was the only offspring of Barry I and Mr Weyerman's female. Favorita I and Toni I are from Sultan and Diana I. Mr Baron Judd gave Sultan I up to me in 1862. From him I obtained Diana I of the St Bernard stock, from which originates my short-haired St Bernard breed of dogs, and from which I have received up to date, with the help of some blood renewal, not only strong and pure, but also improved dogs.

The deterioration of the St Bernard breed of dogs is not only the result of deficiency of kynological skill, and of the difficulty in bringing up the very delicate puppies, but also from financial causes. The majority of owners have made the breeding of these noble animals a trade, and for this reason consider only their own profit. Moreover, foreign buyers desire long-haired animals; so that breeders cross original breeds with long-haired dogs, without making the right choice, only to meet the demand. I do not want to assert that the long-haired St Bernards have depreciated or are less noble, but only that, through faulty or undesirable crossings, and the want of understanding the subject, depreciation has been facilitated. The long-haired St Bernards are, owing to their mass of hair, larger, more imposing, and handsomer (for the long hair can easily cover various shortcomings) than the short-haired, but the latter have the advantage of less perspiration and less covering for vermin, and are more hardy in various climates. For this reason, I have asked the St Bernard Club section of the Swiss Kynological Society to make the breeding of short-haired dogs one of its leading features'.

After giving details of the many dogs from his kennels sold to English breeders, Schumacher concludes:

'Englishmen have drawn their St Bernards from Switzerland, and mostly from well-known breeders, and have not, as the Germans erroneously assert, manufactured the St Bernard breed. To the English belong the merit and honour of first recognising and preferring this breed, and of ennobling it, especially by new blood, by which they have contributed very much to the improvement of the whole race.'

That winning brought its problems, even in those days, we see from the following:

'Before 1867 I learned from an eyewitness that the dogs sold by me won the first prizes in the various dog shows, and I therefore decided to exhibit my dogs at the Paris Show, for which purpose the monks of the St Bernard Hospice gave me a certificate testifying to the purity of my breed, which seems to have contributed to my dogs winning the first prize (the only first prize) during the exhibition Doubt was publicly thrown by an English gentleman on the genuineness of my certificate, and he went specially to the St Bernard Hospice to convince himself on the spot, and after five days he came back converted.'

Dogs change over the years, but exhibitors don't!

The Smooth St Bernard Roland bred in Berne in June 1886 from Belline and an exported son of Ch. Guide.

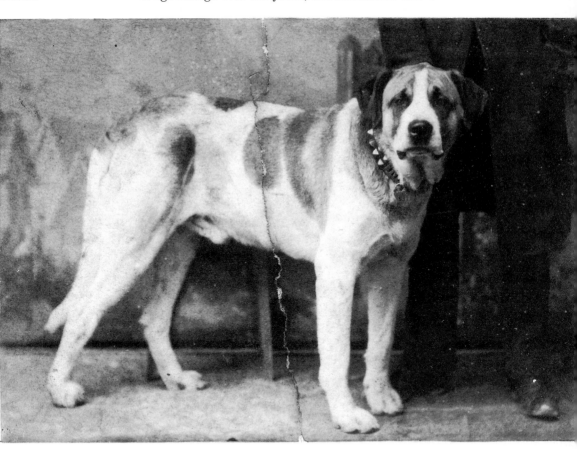

4 Early British St Bernards

The first recorded importation of St Bernards to Britain took place in May 1815, when a Mrs Boode, who lived at Leasowe Castle, near Birkenhead, purchased a dog and bitch from the Hospice. The dog, who was about a year old at the time, was known as Lion. He was smooth-coated, and was said to measure 76 in. long, and stand 31 in. tall at the centre of the back. A painting of him, owned by the Cust family, shows him to have been almost entirely yellow in colour, except for a narrow facial blaze. Early writers state that he was very like a Mastiff, but Manning, writing much later, portrays him as: 'A dog of the short-faced type, with deep square muzzle, strongly-defined stop, massive, well-defined skull, small flat V-shaped ears hung rather high, lots of wrinkle, and correct diamond-shaped eyes, with perfect legs, and well-arched, compact feet.'

Several litters were bred from Lion and the imported bitch, and one of their offspring, a dog named Caesar, is seen on the right of Landseer's famous picture 'The Rescue', painted in 1820. The bitch on the left of the same picture, said to belong to a Mr Christmas, appears to be more of the Mastiff-type, and is less pleasing in colour.

In 1825, there is a record of two more smooth-coated Hospice dogs being imported by Mr John Crabtree, of Kirklees Hall, in Yorkshire, who crossed them with Mastiffs, and it is probable that several others were imported at this time, to strengthen the Mastiff breed. Except for a few, known by name only, there is little information about the imports of this period. In 1827, a bitch, L'Ami, was exhibited at one or two towns, including London. Sir Thomas Lauder, of Berwick, owned a smooth-coated dog named Bass in 1837, and during the 1840s Queen Victoria imported Alp and Glory from the Hospice, having been captivated by the breed during her visit to the Hospice several years beforehand.

In 1854, Mr Albert Smith, a well-known expert on Alpine natural history, owned two St Bernards, together with a pair of Chamois, all of which attracted much publicity. The following extract from the *Illustrated London News* of 3 February 1855 gives a good description of these dogs:

'The St Bernard dogs are male and female. 'Lion' is not pure bred: there is a cross of the English Mastiff about him; but he is much the

'The Resue' by Sir
Edwin Landseer.

finer animal of the two, and very affectionate and gentle, enjoying a romp amazingly. "Diane" is pur sang. She was sent to Mr Albert Smith as a New Year's gift, by the monks last year (but could not start in January for the weather), as an acknowledgment of an increased accession of visitors to the Convent, which they were disposed to think he had induced to go there. The following certificate accompanied her:

Hospice du Grand St Bernard, le 5 Fevrier 1854.

Je soussigné déclare que la chienne, Diane, conduite par le nommé Pierre Francois Favret, de Chamonix, est véritablement de la race des chiens de St Bernard, et qu'elle est conduite à Londres pour Mr Albert Smith.

En foi, MEILLAND, Clavendier.

When Mr Smith was at the Convent, in October last, M. de l'Eglise,

MALE AND FEMALE CHAMOIS, AND ST. BERNARD DOGS, BELONGING TO MR. ALBERT SMITH.

Mr Albert Smith's St Bernard: Diane, imported from the Hospice, and Lion. Reproduced from the *Illustrated London News*, 1855.

the Prior, expressed his great anxiety as to the keeping up of the world-renowned breed. The mortality amongst the dogs had been very great. There were then only two at the Convent: one was a fine light-coloured fellow, very rudely tempered; the other a female, the sister to Mr Smith's Diane, and bearing the same name. The dogs are named, either in allusion to the classical localities of the pass – as Jupiter, Mars, Castor, etc.; or to Napoleon's memorable passage in 1800 – as Drapeau, Marengo, and the like. Fortunately there has been no fatal accident on the mountain since 1851, when the body of a young man was found at Vacherie, a quarter of a mile below the Convent. The improving state of the roads, and the establishment of canteens, have increased the safety of the route. It is not improbable that in a few years there will be a carriageway across the pass. Mr Charles Taylor, of Hollycombe, bought a very fine dog direct from the Convent in 1850. In the event of a breed from this dog and Diane, Mr Smith has promised some puppies to the Monks, a somewhat strange return.'

The use of the term 'St Bernard' in the above is interesting, as, although this name first appeared in 1823, it was not in general use until 1865. The early specimens were known as 'Sacred' or 'Holy' dogs, and then as 'Hospice' dogs, or 'Alpine Mastiffs'.

The two dogs exhibited at Cremorne in 1863 were described as 'Mount St Bernards'. They were both called 'Monk', and were the property of the Revd A. N. Bate and Mr W. H. Stone. They had no pedigrees but were said to be Hospice bred. After this date the breed began to make rapid strides in this country, largely as a result of the efforts of the Revd. J. Cumming Macdona, M. P. This worthy gentleman was a member of the Kennel Club Committee, and as such was entitled to attend shows wearing a silver cross on a crimson ribbon! His kennels at West Kirby in Cheshire, where he was the Rector, housed various breeds, including Pointers, Setters, Fox Terriers, and Pugs. Soon it was not an uncommon sight to see about twenty of his great St Bernards romping together in the sea at West Kirby. In 1866 at the National Show in Birmingham, there was a class for the breed, and Macdona won 1st and 2nd with his Swiss imports, Tell and Bernard.*

Macdona was the first St Bernard fancier in Britain to exhibit stock of his own breeding. Tell, who was a rough-coated red and white dog, had been purchased by Macdona from Herr Schindler of Berne, and was never beaten in the show ring. He sired many puppies, including the rough-coated Molke, who was the male ancestor of the famous 'Save' strain. From his imported bitch, Hedwig, Macdona bred Alp, who was the first British St Bernard exported to the U.S.A. Hope, a fine son of Tell, was presented to the Princess of Wales, later Queen Alexandra.

The Revd. J. Cumming Macdona's Swiss import Tell.

*Tell, who is said to have saved a child from drowning in the River Dee, is still commemorated today, by Tells Tower, the well-known West Kirby landmark, which Macdona built in memory of his famous dog.

Another St Bernard breeder of importance at this time was Mr J. H. Murchison, a prominent exhibitor of Fox Terriers, and also a member of the Kennel Club Committee. From Heinrich Schumacher's kennels he imported the rough-coated dog, Thor, whose pedigree appears on page 168. Although he failed in head, Thor was much used at stud. From Macdona, Murchison purchased the dog, Monarque, whom Schumacher had bred from Sultan I and Diana I.

In 1870, Sir Charles Isham imported from Mr Egger of Kandersteg a large rough-coated dog known as Leo, who was white with brindle markings. Leo was believed to carry some Mastiff blood, but his influence on the breed was far-reaching. He was mated to Mr Frederick Gresham's Bernie, a daughter of Macdona's Bernard. Mr Gresham's account of the union and its results makes interesting reading:

'Bernie was allowed to run about at her own sweet will, until she was three years old, when it occurred to me that, as St Bernards were then becoming popular, I might turn her to good account. But how to make a start was the question and where to find a sire not too far from home. Leo was the property of Sir Charles Isham, Lamport Hall, Northamptonshire. Matters were however arranged by the intervention of friends, and the remuneration of a guinea to be presented to an Orphan Asylum. In due course, a family of fourteen arrived, Bernie having selected a standing in a stable for her nursery. The whelps seemed to be all colours, one a white, another a black. Ignorant of the correct colour of St Bernards, I consulted my groom, and was relieved of my anxiety when I heard that the white puppy was somewhat like Leo. The order was, pick out the six biggest and put the other eight into a bucket – they cannot all be kept! Fortunately the black, and also the white puppy were among the six biggest. The former lived to be the rough-coated Champion Monk, and the latter Champion Abbess, who was smooth-coated. Another guinea's worth from Bernie produced a litter of seventeen, making thirty-one puppies in less than twelve months. The bucket was not brought into requisition this time.'

Abbess, who was a smooth-coated bitch, standing 30½ in. at shoulder and weighing 150 lb, had many offspring, and exerted a considerable influence on the breed. In 1875, her mating to Molke, the son of Macdona's Tell, gave rise to the 'Save' strain, from which came numerous winners. Her mating to Murchison's Thor, imported from Schumacher, produced Champions Hector, The Shah, Dagmar, and Abbess II, all in one litter.

The following extract from a show catalogue of 1873, reproduced by courtesy of Mrs Walker, indicates the tremendous upsurge of interest in the breed at this time, and the high prices even then being asked by top breeders:

Extract from Catalogue of Grand National Exhibition, held at the Crystal Palace in June 1873

ST. BERNARDS (ROUGH & SMOOTH COATED) FOR DOGS ONLY
Champion Classes (for previous winners of Three First Prizes at any Shows)

CLASS 9   ROUGH-COATED
(**PRIZE:** a piece of plate, valued £8.0.0.

94	Mr. David Elphinstone Seton Imported from Switzerland. Not for sale.	MENTHON	Age 5 years 11 months
95	J.H. Murchinson Esq., F.R.G.S. Breeder: Rev. J.C. Macdona. By Gessler-Hedwig. Not for sale	APL	Age 5 years

CLASS 10   SMOOTH-COATED
PRIZE: a piece of plate, value £8.0.0.

96	J.H. Murchinson Esq., F.R.G.S. Breeder: H. Schumacher. By Souldon. Not for sale.	MONARQUE	Age 6 years 3 months

CLASS 11   ST. BERNARDS (ROUGH-COATED) DOGS & BITCHES
First PRIZE: a piece of plate, value £8.0.0.
Second PRIZE: a piece of plate, value £4.0.0.

97	Jose Merino Ballesteros, K.G.C.T.C., F.S.A.	URSA	Age 2 years
98	Mr. David Elphinstone Seton Not for sale.	FRANCE	Age 5 years
99	Mr. David Elphinstone Seton Not for sale	TIRASSE	Age 1 year 7 months
100	Mr. George James Playfair Price 14 guineas	BARRIS	Age 2 years 3 months
101	Mr. James Porter Imported. Not for sale.	VIC	Age 2 years 8 months
102	Miss Hales Imported. Not for sale.	JURA	Age 3 years 6 months
103	Mr. William Alfred Joyce Imported. Not for sale	BERRY	Age 4 years 4 months
104	Mr. William Alfred Joyce By Sir Charles Isham's Leo- dam by Mr. Stone's Barry. Not for sale	QUEEN BERTHA	Age 1 year 11 months
105	Mr. Richard Simmonds Price £210	MACKNEY	Age 2 years 6 months
106	Mr. Andrew Pears By Mr. Bradshaw's Barry-Norma By Mr. Sydney's Leo-Mount-Tell -Juno	BARRY	Age 19 months
107	Mr. C. Ellerby Imported. Price £25	WALLACE	Age 11 months
108	Mr. William Wilberforce Baynes Breeder: Mr. Cochat. Price £250	TURC	Age 2 years last August
109	Mr. Elise Marquardt Not for sale	ROLAND	Age 3 years

110	Major Robert S. Rous	SAXON	Age 2 years 8 months
	Breeder: Mr. Best. Price £200		
111	J.H. Murchison Esq., F.R.G.S.	MENTOR	Age 11 months 3 days
	Breeder: Rev. F.C. Hope-Grant.		
	By H.R.H. the Prince of Wales's		
	Hope-Hedwig. Not for sale.		

CLASS 12 ST. BERNARDS (SMOOTH-COATED) DOGS & BITCHES

First PRIZE: a piece of plate, value £8.0.0.
Second PRIZE: a piece of plate, value £4.0.0.

112	Mr. Percy G. Young	CARLO	Age 2 years 1 month
	Imported. Not for sale.		
113	Mr. James Clarke	BURNIE	Age 1 year 9 months
	Breeder: Exhibitor. Price £50		
114	Mr. Fred Gresham	BRUCE	Age 2 years 1 month
	Breeder: Exhibitor. By Sir Chas.		
	Isham's Leo- Bernie. Price		
	11 guineas		
115	Mr Fred Gresham	BELLA	Age 2 years 6 months
	Breeder T.J. Hooper, Esq., By		
	Mr. Hooper's Barry. Price 11		
	guineas.		
117	Miss Aglionby	JURA	Age 2 years 11 months
	Bred by the monks of St.		
	Bernard. Price £200.		
118	Mr. James Churton	TIGER	Age 2 years 3 months
	Breeder: Mr. James McLauglin.		
	By Pluto-Mona, both imported.		
	Price £60.		
119	Mr. Augustus Smith	MONK	Age 2 years 3 months
	Bred by the Monks of St.		
	Bernard. Not for sale.		
120	Mr. George Swan Nottage	BARRY	Age 3 years
	Bred at the Monastery of St.		
	Bernard. Not for sale.		
121	Mr. Henry Wilson Price	CAESAR	Age 2 years 8 months
122	J.M. Murchison, Esq., F.R.G.S.	CONSTANCE	Age 10 months
	Breeder: Exhibitor. By		
	Vansittart's dog ex-owner's Jura		
123	J.H. Murchinson Esq., F.R.G.S.	JURA	Age 3 years
	Breeder: Rev. J.C. Maxdona. By		
	Monarque-Jungfrau. Not for sale.		
124	Mr. George Forbes	DRAGON	Age 2 years 10 months
	Bred by the Monks of the		
	Hospice of the Great St.Bernard		
	Not for sale.		
125	Rev J.C. Macdona	MADCHEN	Age 1 year 9 months
	Bred by the Monks of St.		
	Bernard. Winner of the 1st Prize		
	and extra as best in six classes		
	at Henley, and second at		
	Glasgow 1873, the only times		
	exhibited. Price £1000. In pup to		
	Oscar, by Monarque-Jungfrau.		

RESULTS
Class 9   Prize 95
Class 10   Prize 96
Class 11   First Prize 111
Class 11   Second 103
Class 11   H.C. 99
Class 12   First Prize 125
Class 12   Second 117
Class 12   H. C. 118
Class 12   H. C. 123

After these beginnings, the breed in this country went from strength to strength. Prominent exhibitors of the 1870s were Mr J. F. Smith of Sheffield and Mr S. W. Smith of Leeds. The 1880s saw another tremendous boom in the breed, and by combination of the Thor, Leo and Tell strains, many fine St Bernards were produced. Mr S. W. Smith's Rector, who was reported to have stood 34 in. at shoulder, was sold to America for £300, a high price in those days. Mr J. F. Smith's Champion Save (pedigree on page 168), a bright chestnut dog, with correct white markings and black shadings, was said to weight 190 lb and to combine the best features of the Tell and Leo strains. Dr Russell's Cadwallader was another big winner of this period. Perhaps the most famous of all was Mr J. F. Smith's Bayard, a grandson of Thor on both sides of his pedigree, who had more Championships to his name than any other dog of the time, except Plinlimmon, his grandson. Bayard's great-great-grandmother was said to have been a Mastiff, and he occasionally transmitted Mastiff colouring to his offspring.

Plinlimmon was the property of the Revd Arthur Carter, who had purchased him in the North of England as a puppy. He was of gigantic weight and height, and, after changing hands several times, was finally sold to America for 7,000 dollars, where he became the property of an actor, Mr Emmett, who exhibited him in theatres.

The high prices that could be obtained in America for the 'giants' of the British show ring appears at this time to have led to a craze for size among the breeders in this country, and the breed began to deteriorate, as type and soundness were disregarded at the expense of great weight and stature.

One of the 'giants', Sir Bedivere, who weighed 212 lb and stood 33½ in. at shoulder, was unbeaten in this country. His owner, Mr T. H. Green, sold him to America for £1300, where he finally met his match in another British export, Princess Florence, who was said to weigh 223 lb. Sadly, very few of the high-priced stock sent to America survived for very long, but whether this was due to the climate being too hot for them, as is often stated, or because their vast weights led to physical degeneration, is a matter for conjecture.

The Revd. Arthur
Carter's Smooth
bitch Thisbe, bred
from Alpenstock III
and Diane.

Although a standard of points for the breed was drawn up in 1886 by
the Revd Arthur Carter and Mr Frederick Gresham, which does not
differ significantly from our present official Kennel Club Standard, it
did little to halt the decline in quality which occurred during the
closing years of the last century. Once size began to take precedence
over beauty and soundness, the breed began to lose its appeal to the

ROUGH ST BERNARD CH. "SIR BEDIVERE" S. SMITH OWNER.

The famous Sir Bedivere, considered a 'giant' in his day, although only 33 in. in height. He was sold to America for a record price.

general public. The essential benevolent expression began to disappear, and faulty conformation, especially in the hind-quarters, became common. Another factor, leading to physical problems, was the over-short muzzle, which had been favoured as a way of giving the impression of width and depth to the foreface.

One of the few far-sighted breeders of the time, Mrs Jaggers, wrote: 'There are signs that the St Bernard is waning in public favour. This may be only a passing cloud, and perhaps when the dog is bred more to original type, he will again become first favourite among canine pets.'

Mrs Jaggers, and one or two other breeders at the turn of the century, was not influenced by the current craze for size at the expense of soundness. The rough dog, Pouf, owned by Mr H. W. Roberts, was a small, compact animal, with a fine head and muzzle. He was used widely at stud, and his offspring were of outstanding quality. Belline, a smooth bitch bred in Murren, and a descendent of Schumacher's Sultan I, produced two notable sons, Guide and Sans Peur, and several notable grandchildren, including the fine smooth dog, Watch. It was on the 'Pouf', 'Belline', and 'Save' strains that future breeders based their efforts to bring the breed back to its former quality and eminence.

5 Twentieth-Century British St Bernards

A milestone in the history of St Bernards in this country was reached in 1896 when Dr George Inman and Mr Ben Walmsley formed a partnership and established their famous Bowden kennels, first at Barford in Somerset, and finally at Bowden Priory in Cheshire. Dr Inman had owned good dogs for several years, and set about breeding on scientific lines. He is said to have crossed a Smooth bitch, Kenilworth, with a brindle Mastiff, and then crossed the progeny back to his St Bernards, with most successful results. The Bowden kennels soon produced a series of winners which were almost invincible in the show ring, being noted for their grand head-type and superb soundness. No unsound animals were ever exhibited or used for breeding. Among the well-known winners bred at Bowden were the dogs Tannhauser (a Rough who won 16 C. C.s) and Viking (a Smooth with 12 C.C.s). Two of their bitches, the rough Judith Inman, and the Smooth Viola, each took 14 C. C.s. The Bowden kennels at one time housed no less than twelve home-bred Champions. It was written of the partnership:

> 'This firm established a race of dogs as sound as Terriers, big and massive in size, with head the chiselling and grandeur of which even their greatest enemies were ultimately constrained to admit. With the exception of one dog, probably, there was no trace of Mastiff, or any other alien cross. Their enormously deep, square forefaces, nice stops, beautifully chiselled skulls, pellucid eyes, and benevolent expression, denoting beautiful dispositions, which all the dogs possessed, were at once the admiration and marvel of the fancy.'

The Bowden partnership ended with Dr Inman's death abroad, and the Bowden stock was distributed throughout the country. In one sense, this dispersal was of benefit to the breed, as it gave new heart to exhibitors from other kennels, who for many years had been overshadowed by the Bowden dominance.

One of the greatest successes of this period fell to Ch. The Pride of Sussex, winner of 23 C.C.s, who in 1912 was Best in Show at Cruft's

Left. Mr J. Proctor's Ch. Viola (1900). This famous Smooth bitch, bred by Messrs Inman and Walmesley, was the winner of 14 C.Cs.

Right. Mr G. Sinclair's Ch. Lord Montgomery was Champion at the Crystal Palace and Edinburgh in 1906.

and Birmingham. This famous Rough dog was a son of Ch. Lord Montgomery, who was by the noted Ch. Tannhauser. His owner, Mr H. Stocken, writing in 1913, after judging the Thirty-Second St Bernard Club Show, defended the breed against accusations of deterioration:

'Well, I have heard a lot about the deterioration of this breed, but in my opinion it is in as good a way now as it has ever been since I have been exhibiting. With a bitch like Ch. Destiny of Duffryn, and a dog like Ch. The Pride of Sussex to lead the breed, how can people talk as I have heard them? No St Bernard has ever done what these two have done, and if the breed has so deteriorated, well, then, all other breeds must be very bad indeed, and I think we can safely leave these 'croakers' to get what consolation they can out of this. Again, there is no getting away from the fact that at the present time the dogs exhibited are, with few exceptions, sound, and when I started exhibiting they were just the opposite, it being the exception to find sound dogs. I well remember a remark I heard made at the ringside by an onlooker that they wanted "a wheelbarrow to bring the dogs into the ring!". Now, this cannot be said at the present time, and is, in my opinion, one of the reasons that the breed is holding its own.'

Some of the Bowden dogs found their way to the celebrated Pearl Kennels of Mr and Mrs J. Redwood, who had one of the few kennels to survive World War I. This hit the breed hard, as food was scarce, and only a nucleus of Saints remained when breeding operations recommenced after the war. Mr and Mrs Redwood continued to breed many noted winners, and a total of 42 Champions carried their prefix.

Mrs A. Parker's Ch. Chrysantheme. Bred by Messrs Inman and Walmesley from Ch. Egmont and Nameless.

H. B. Hewitt's Ch. Peter the Great (1910), a grandson of Ch. Tannhauser on both sides of his pedigree.

Left: The Smooth, King of Northumbria, widely used at stud after World War I, and grandsire of Mrs K. Staines's Ch. Bernardo.

Below: The late Mr J. Redwood with one of his 42 Pearl Champions.

Left: Mr J. Brearley's Ch. St. Gerald Pearl, bred in 1927, shows the head properties typical of this period.

Right: Mr J. Redwood's Ch. Sabrina Pearl. Bred in 1929 from St Jerome Pearl and St Ethel Pearl: a good-headed bitch with poor conformation.

Mrs K. Staines's Abbotspass Kennels were founded in 1922 at Reigate, in Surrey, and her kennel buildings were reputed to be the best in the country. Her foundation stock included Ch. Bernado and Nerissa, who were litter brother and sister, and were bred by Mr E. Chasty from Ch. The King's Daughter and St Benedick Pearl. Mrs Staines's aim was to get away from the Pearl strain and start a new line, and her first major success was Ch. Bassanio. She imported stock from Switzerland to give much needed new bloodlines. Her most famous winner was Ch. Abbotspass Romeo, for whom she is said to have refused offers of up to £2,000.

The only adult male ever to be sold by Mrs Staines was Ch. Abbotspass Friar, who was acquired by Mr Mellor; this dog was line bred to Ch. Sebastian Pearl, a descendant of the Bowden line. The somewhat doubtful honour of owning what was said to be the biggest bitch ever shown went to Mr Chasty, whose Lady Molly won the bitch C.C. at Cruft's in 1932, and was said to weigh 15 stone.

Apart from some of the noted dogs of Mrs Staines's, the standard of the breed during the 1920s and early '30s was generally very low, and it was said that a dog might, at that time, be so weak in leg bone as to be a complete cripple, yet win the highest honours.

Mrs Staines did not allow her dogs to be placed at public stud, and so did little to improve the general standard of the breed outside her own kennel. In accordance with instructions in her will, all her St Bernards were destroyed immediately after her death, so the Abbotspass blood was lost completely.

At one time a group of contemporary breeders very much wished to

Above: Ch Bernado, bred in 1922, was one of the first St Bernards owned by Mrs K. Staines.

Above Right: Mr H. Mellor's Ch. Abbotspass Friar, bred by Mrs K. Staines in 1928 from King Boris and Abbotspass Margaret.

Right: Mrs K. Staines's Ch. Abbotspass Portia, bred in 1929. A Saint with such obvious head faults would not win in the ring today.

Below: Mrs K. Staines and her kennelmen exercise a group of the famous Abbotspass St Bernards. Ch. Abbotspass Romeo is in the foreground.

use one of Mrs Staines's champions; the good lady was known to have a kennelman who was somewhat over-fond of his liquor, so the said breeders took the trouble to discover the whereabouts of his favourite 'local', and waylaid him there. After plying him with drink, they persuaded him to agree to an illicit union, which took place next morning during a detour on his walk with the dogs. Puppies were duly born, and bore such a striking resemblance to their famous sire that Mrs Staines discovered the truth and sacked the unfortunate kennelman.

Of much significance to the bloodlines of the future were the efforts of the Misses Pratt, who inherited a fortune and decided to spend it on St Bernards. They set up their Berndean kennels at Newton Mearns in Renfrewshire, and imported several Saints from Switzerland. In 1932 they mated their imported bitch Emira Flora to Ch. Moorgate Masterpiece and bred the lovely Berndean Ailsa, an almost all-white bitch, and the Rough dog Ch. The Marquis of Wetterhorn. A subsequent mating of Ailsa to Mrs J. F. Briggs's Ch. Beldene Bruno produced Ch. Berndean Invader. Another of the Pratts's Swiss imports, Berndean Prinz Von Rigi, was mated to Monte Rosa, a daughter of St Silverias Pearl, and produced Jupiter of Priorsleigh, owned by Mrs Cox. A second mating of Monte Rosa, this time to The Alpine Colossus, gave rise to Fabius of Priorsleigh, the sire of Mrs Brigg's Beldene Barco. Almost without exception, the pedigree of the post-war St Bernards can be traced back to these dogs, and tables showing the lines to which they gave rise can be found in the Appendix.

Above: Scottish St Bernards of the thirties: Miss G. R. Pratt with (left to right) Schweizer Cuno, Emira Flora (both Swiss imports), Ch. Berndean Ailsa, and Ch. Berndean Roderick.

The World War II made it almost impossible to feed even one St Bernard, yet a nucleus of dedicated breeders managed to keep small kennels going, and when hostilities ceased, the breed made a remarkable comeback. One whose kennels had been destroyed by a shell was Mrs Graydon Bradley of Dover, but her Boystown St Bernards soon began to re-establish themselves in the ring. She worked closely with Scottish breeder Miss J. Fyffe, whose Panbride St Bernards were well-known.

The first post-war Champion was Yew Tree St Christopher, bred by Mrs C. Walker (later Mrs C. Hutchings) of the Christcon prefix. Owned by Mr A. K. Gaunt, St Christopher was a grandson of Jupiter of Priorsleigh on the sire's side, and Ch. Berndean Invader on the dam's. He was the first of 61 British Champions to be made up by Mr Gaunt, of whom almost half were home-bred. Mr and Mrs Gaunt had begun breeding St Bernards in the mid-thirties under the prefix Twokays, which they later changed to Cornagarth. Their first bitch Champion, bred by Mr T. Lightfoot, was Cornagarth Wendy of Flossmere, a daughter of Jupiter of Priorsleigh: her dam was Prudence of Priorsleigh, by Ch. Berndean Invader.

Mr A. K. Gaunt was Secretary of the English St Bernard Club for 27 years, and exerted a dominating influence on the breed throughout this period. Ably assisted by his wife Kathleen, he made the Cornagarth St Bernards world-famous, though his kennel facilities at Ripley in Derbyshire were extremely limited. It is undoubtedly true to say that Cornagarth was to the post-war St Bernard what Bowden, Pearl and Abbotspass had been to successive generations in the past.

The Cornagarth dogs were noted for their outstanding head properties and massive bone and substance. Their expression and temperament were the epitome of benevolence, but some were not as strong in hind-quarters as one would have wished. The Swiss dog, Marshall Von Zwing Uri, was acquired by the Gaunts in 1952, having been brought into this country by a returning serviceman, and his name appears in many of today's pedigrees. During the late 1950s Mr Gaunt worked in close collaboration with Mrs G. Slazenger of the Durrowabbey St Bernards, and eleven Champions carried the joint Cornagarth–Durrowabbey prefixes. Following the deaths of Mr and Mrs Gaunt, the Cornagarth kennel was dispersed, and the type which it stamped so markedly on the breed is already being changed.

The other outstanding kennel of the early post-war period was that of Mrs R. L. Walker of Thringstone in Leicestershire. Mrs Walker, who had owned St Bernards since the end of the last century, began to show her dogs shortly after World War II. Her first Champion was Ch. St. Dominic of Brenchley, and a series of eighteen others followed, almost without exception home-bred. With the help of her twin sons

Left: the late Mr A. K. Gaunt with the first two post-war champions: Ch. Cornagarth Wendy of Flossmere (Jupiter of Priorsleigh ex Prudence of Priorsleigh) and Ch. Yew Tree St Christopher (Yew Tree St Bruno ex Yew Tree St Filumena).

Mrs E. Graydon Bradley and a group of her Boystown St Bernards in 1950.

Gilbert and Eric, she produced in her Peldartor kennels a number of tall, powerful dogs with outstanding heads and muzzles. Among the most notable were the Smooth dog Ch. Colossus of Peldartor and the Rough bitch Ch. Carol of Peldartor, whose son, Ch. Peldartor Orrangit, was Best of Breed at Cruft's in 1956. Mrs Walker retained her interest until the time of her death in 1981 at the age of ninety-five. Her son Mr G. Walker was Secretary of the United St Bernard Club for 17 years, and in this capacity did much to encourage new exhibitors.

The noted Burtonswood Kennel of Miss M. Hindes came to the fore at the end of the fifties. Her many Champions to date have included the celebrated Ch. Burtonswood Bossy Boots who won Best in Show at Crufts in 1974. Boots sired at least fifteen British champions and numerous overseas title holders.

Another St Bernard to do well at Crufts was Ch. Snowranger Cascade, owned by Mrs J. McMurray. He won the Working Group in 1976. A noted breeder of the fifties was the late Mrs E. Muggleton, who built up her well-known Bernmont Kennels with the help of her daughter, Miss P. Muggleton, who is the present Secretary of the English St Bernard Club. One of their famous dogs was Ch. Bernmont Warlord, who won the Working Group at Bath in 1969.

During the sixties, there were further imports from Europe, including the Swiss dog, Ch. Tello Von Saulient, which Mrs C. Bradley and Mr P. Hill introduced into their Snowranger Kennels in Buckinghamshire. The import in 1969 of an in-whelp bitch from Germany had a very important influence on breed type. Of her litter born in

Top Winners at Crufts in 1955. Mr W. Townley with Ch. What a Girl and Mrs E. Graydon Bradley with Boystown Sir Galahad. The judge is Mr W. D. Joslin.

Above Left: An example of an early Cornagarth dog, Ch. Cornagarth Cornborrow St. Oliver was Best in Show at Birmingham in 1950.

Above Right: Ch. Cornagarth Marshall Von Zwing Uri. This Swiss import of the early 1950s was widely used by Mr A. K. Gaunt in his breeding programme.

Right: Mrs R. L. Walker's Ch. Carol of Peldartor, by Beldene Mickado ex Cornagarth Dawn. Best St Bernard Bitch at Cruft's in 1953.

Below Right: Ch Peldartor Rosseau (1958), by Ch Peldartor Charnwood Bruno ex Peldartor Anka V. D. Schlense. Owned and bred by Mrs R. L. Walker.

Below Left: Mrs R. L. Walker's Ch. Peldartor Reubens (1966), by Ch. Peldartor Xcellence ex Ch. Peldartor Julich.

quarantine, one dog, Daphnydene Karro Von Birkenkopf, became a champion in the ownership of Mrs D. Ayckbourne. Karro's litter brother, Cornagarth Kuno Von Birkenkopf, was purchased by Mr Gaunt, and is an ancestor of the majority of present day British Saints. He was used extensively at stud, and sired eleven champions, including Ch. Burtonswood Bossy Boots.

The publicity given to Bossy Boot's Crufts success appeared to bring about a great increase in the popularity of the St Bernard. Breed registrations rose from 376 in 1970 to a peak of 988 in 1979. A sudden influx of this nature is undesireable in any breed, suggesting as it does the wish of certain breeders to cash in on increased demand, rather than to improve the breed. Happily, the high figures have not been maintained, the number registered in 1986 being 486.

To keep pace with increased registrations, the number of sets of Challenge Certificates available to St Bernards also rose to new heights. In 1969, 14 sets were on offer, while for 1989 the breed has been allocated 33 sets, an increase of 146%. Among the leading winners of the last decade have been Mr and Mrs J. Harpham's Whaplode St Bernards. Their Ch. Whaplode Unique amassed a total of 22 CCs, and is the breed record holder. His daughter, Ch. Lucky Charm of Whaplode holds the breed record for bitches with 20 CCs to her credit. Another frequent winner was Mrs G. Topping's Ch. Topvalley Wogan's Winner who won 19 CCs.

Below Left: Ch. Cornagarth Burtonswood Be Great. Bred by Miss M. Hindes, and the last of 61 Champions made up by the late Mr A. K. Gaunt.

Below Right: Ch. Burtonwood Bossy Boots by Cornagarth Kuno Von Birkenopf ex Ch. Burtonswood Beloved. Best in Show, Cruft's, 1974. Owned and bred by Miss M. Hindes.

Above Left: Mrs J. McMurray's Ch Snowranger Cascade. Winner of the Working
Group at Cruft's in 1975.

Above Right: Ch. Snowranger Chloris. Bred
and owned by Mrs C. Bradley and Mr P. Hill;
Cruft's C.C. winner in 1968.

Left: Mrs E. and Miss P. H. Muggleton's Ch.
Bernmont Warlord, winner of 8 Challenge
Certificates and the Working Group at Bath in
1969.

Below Left: Mrs D. Ayckbourne's Ch. Daph-
nydene Karro Von Birkenopf, imported from
Germany and *Below Right* his litter brother
A. K. Gaunt's Cornagarth Kuno Von Birken
Kopf.

The number of Smooth Saints exhibited in this country remains disappointingly small, but there have been some good specimens produced in recent years. Mr and Mrs M. Wensley have been great Smooth enthusiasts and have made up several champions in this variety, including Ch. Swindridge Sir Dorian, Ch. Swindridge Ferdinand and Ch. Swindridge Matthew, in direct line from one another. Well known Smooth bitches have been Mrs M. Gwilliam's Ch. Be Elect of Burtonswood, Mr and Mrs D. Owen's Ch. Coatham Gin N Tonic and Mr and Mrs P. Girling's Ch. Swindridge Laura.

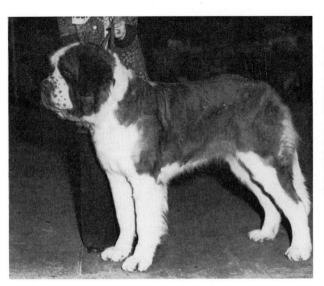

Above Left: Mrs M. Gwilliam's Ch. Coatham Star Shine, by Ch. Burtonwood Black Tarquin ex Northam Star of Coatham. Cruft's C.C. winner in 1976 and 1977.

Above right: The author's Ch. Lindenhall High Commissioner, winner of fourteen Challenge Certificates and the Working Group at Dumfries in 1974.

Left: Mrs J. McMurray's Ch. Alpentire Paters Princess (1977), winner of eight Challenge Certificates.

The late Mrs A. K. Gaunt, with Ch. Cornagarth Stroller, and the author with Gershwin Melody. C.C. winners at Blackpool in 1968 under Mr W. Burrow.

It is impossible to mention all the leading winners by name, and a list of all British Champions since 1947, together with details of their breeding and ownership will be found in the Appendix. It is plain that recent import of dogs from the continent is leading to much greater diversification of type, and new people, taking up the breed, are finding it difficult to determine what should be the correct type. It seems probable that the growing cost and shortage of food will make it increasingly difficult to feed large dogs, and that the big kennel of St Bernards, with its own distinctive breeding strain, will become a feature of the past.

Below left: Ch. Whaplode Unique owned by Mr and Mrs J. Harpham. The winner of 22 Challenge Certificates, a record for the breed.

Below right: Miss L. E. Cooper's Ch. Merridale Bouncer winner of the Working Group at Bath in 1985.

6 St Bernards of Other Nations

It is universally acknowledged that the British breeders of the late nineteenth century must take the credit for developing the St Bernard from working dog to show dog. These pioneers of the breed in our country decided, unfortunately perhaps, not to adopt the Standard drawn up by the International Congress at Zurich in 1822, although a delegate from this country, H. Inman Betterton, attended the conference. Since this time, Britain has been the only country not to conform to the International Standard, and this dissension has not fostered good-will with breeders abroad. English breeders have been only too ready to use as out-crosses the various continental dogs imported into this country; there can, for instance, be scarcely a pedigree of a dog living today in Britain which does not contain the name of the German import Cornagarth Kuno Von Birkenkopf.

Interpretation of the Standard, and emphasis placed on its various aspects, may be a matter of disagreement, but breeders of all countries should try to recognise merit where it exists elsewhere, and to work together for the international advancement of our noble breed. The St Bernard is universally loved and admired, and it would seem that its interests could now best be served by dropping the somewhat insular approach of our forefathers. Although this is primarily a book for British breeders, it would not be complete without a brief survey of the St Bernard scene throughout the world.

Europe
With no quarantine barriers between the various European countries, much interchange of stock and studs, can and does occur. This, together with the practice of interchanging judges between shows in the various countries, has led to the emergence of much similarity of type in the Saints throughout the continent.

SWITZERLAND
The Swiss St Bernard Club was set up in 1884, and numerous breeders carried on the work begun thirty years before by Henri Schumacher. Foremost among them at this time was Dr Kuenzli of Gallen, who had

a kennel of about eighty dogs, which he boarded out at neighbouring farms. He based his work on the Hospice dog, and tried to combine the best qualities of this with the line evolved by Schumacher. He sought good conformation and movement, and used to say that a St Bernard should 'stand like a horse'. His most famous dog was Kean I, who was outstanding in head properties, and is still regarded as a model for the breed overseas.

Another great pioneer of the breed in Switzerland was Major Bloesch, of Biel, who sought to increase the size of his dogs by importing stock from England. He aimed for larger and more expressive heads, which the English breeders had neglected. He was so successful that a great number of his Saints were eventually sold back to England.

Throughout the years Swiss breeders have made steady progress. There has been little disagreement on type, and a very high standard of judging. During the war years the Swiss kennels did not suffer the set-backs of those in England and Germany.

After the World War II, the famous Kennel Zwing Uri, at Fluelen, overlooking Lake Lucerne, became a noted tourist attraction, and its exports were world-wide. The dog, Marshall Von Zwing Uri, had a marked influence on the breed in England. Another famous name is that of Von Saulient, the prefix of Ed Rodel, from whence came the English import, Tello Von Saulient. In 1970, of the ninety litters bred in Switzerland, eighteen were produced in the Von Saulient Kennels, eight at the Hospice, and, of the remainder, 59 came from kennels which only produced one litter during the year. Although Herr Rodel's kennel is now so dominant, he began his career as a breeder almost by chance, having purchased a St Bernard for his farm shortly after the war. This bitch whelped a litter of 'St Bernard' puppies to a neighbour's dog, and they sold so quickly that their owner decided to take up the breed seriously, and now has a kennel of about sixty dogs.

Doyen of the breed in Switzerland until his recent death was Dutchman Albert de la Rie. His book *One Hundred Years of the St Bernard* is a classic, and he enjoyed a world-wide reputation as an International Judge and expert on the breed.

GERMANY

Early pioneers of the St Bernard in Germany imported stock from England and Switzerland to lay the foundations of the breed in their country. Perhaps the most famous was Dr Caster of Winkle Rheingau, who also bred Great Danes. He was instrumental in setting up the German St Bernard Club in 1891. The Club originally had sixty members, and, as many came from the Bavarian region, the new organisation was based in Munich. Caster's kennel was not large, but he imported stock from England in preference to Switzerland, as he believed that the English breeders, having been willing to pay astronomical prices for their foundation stock, had acquired the very best. In Caster's day, most of the German dogs were Roughs, and were known as Alpenhunde.

Prince Albrecht of Solms had one of the largest early kennels on the continent. From England he imported the Smooth dog Courage, who was a great show specimen but disappointing at stud. He was a greyish-white dog, with yellow patches, and though reported to have stood 35½ in. at the shoulder, he weighed only 140 lb, so must have been somewhat lightly built.

Thirty-six St Bernards were entered at the Hanover All-Breed Show in 1882, but only six were considered 'pure bred'. The judge was an Englishman who placed some of the mongrels among his winners, which did not please the German breeders. An English import, Cadwallader, was Best of Breed, while Gessler, owned by the Prince of Solms, was placed second.

During the years following the Hanover show, interest in St Bernards grew in Germany, with many new breeders entering the ranks. It is said that indiscriminate crossing led to some fall in quality. The Altona kennel, founded by Ludwig Kaston in 1897, was one of the most noted, and helped the breed to survive the World War I. Max Nather took over the direction of the German St Bernard Club in 1903 and was responsible for its Stud Book and publications until 1938. Many outstanding specimens were bred in the Grossglockner Kennels, of Hans Glockner, who ran the Club from 1938 to 1950 and maintained interest in the breed against great odds during the World War II. Another great German breeder, Alois Schmid, learned much from Glockner, and his Bismarckturm St Bernards began to come to the fore during the thirties. His motto, 'A good breeder lives for his dogs, not on them,' could be more widely followed.

The Nazis tried to interfere with the breeding of St Bernards, as they wished the Alsatian to be regarded as Germany's National Dog. The S. S. publications printed articles criticising the shape of the head and eyes as indicating viciousness, and the Nazis forbade the awarding of the titles Club Champion and International Champion. However, at the beginning of the war, they were only too ready to train St Bernards as rescue dogs for use in Alpine conditions.

The war and its aftermath inevitably harmed the breed greatly, and at the time when money was almost useless, German Saints were even bartered to buy food. Like the nation itself, the breed in Germany has made a remarkable recovery since the war, and German kennels now house some of the finest dogs in Europe. In order to achieve quality in preference to quantity, the German Club places certain restrictions on

A top winning European St Bernard, German Champion Omar V. Roscuckellar. Europa Sieger 1975 and 1977.

breeders; only six puppies in any one litter may be registered, and the rest must be destroyed. A dog must be at least two years old before being used at stud, and a bitch, twenty months. The breed club is one of the strongest and most active in Europe, and has well over a thousand members.

EAST GERMANY
The breed has many enthusiasts behind the Iron Curtain, but communication and exchange of stock is difficult to achieve. There is a flourishing St Bernard Club in Dresden, and great interest in the breed.

ITALY
When Italian St Bernards are mentioned, the name of Dr Antonio Morsiani is synonymous with them. Dr Morsiani has devoted a lifetime to the breed, and has built up one of the finest kennels in the world at Ravenna. His aim has been to restore size to the breed, and he has imported stock from Germany and Switzerland to achieve his aim. One of his most famous dogs was the Swiss import, Ch. Anton Von Hofli, who died in 1969, and was the sire of the great Ch. Lorenz Von

Above Left: The Smooth bitch, Italian Ch. Alma Del Soccorso, owned by Dr Antonio Morsiani, shows the head qualities favoured by this noted continental breeder.

Above Right: Dr Morsiani's International Ch. Rex Del Soccorso.

Liebiwil, who stood 36½ in. at the shoulder. Winners from his Del Soccorso Kennels carry all before them in the show ring in Italy. Dr Morsiani is President of the Italian St Bernard Club, which has over a hundred members.

FRANCE

By comparison with other major European countries, the breed is numerically weak in France, although the French have their own Breed Club. In 1971, fifteen Saints were exhibited at the Paris Show, but entries at other shows during that year failed to reach double figures. In the following year, Paris entries numbered eighteen, but there were many absentees. An English observer reported that on this occasion it seemed that a disproportionate amount of time was spent in examining the teeth of each exhibit, and in the case of one dog, the judge had to be assisted by four men in order to do so. Many of the exhibits were of Swiss or German breeding. Best dog was Porthos du Clos du Petit Saint Bernard, owned by M. Choppe, who was then the Secretary of the French Club.

DENMARK

The first St Bernard to reach Denmark was Trilby, a descendant of Schumacher's Sultan I. In 1900 there were 31 registrations. Pioneer of the breed was C. F. Bardino, of Christiansbjerg, Arhus, whose first

Champion, Donnar Von Donaubastion, had been bred in Germany in 1921. There is now much enthusiasm for the breed in Denmark, the Danes favouring dark-masked dogs with good action. The Danish St Bernard Club was founded in 1973, and a number of Danish Saints have been exported to the U.S.A. Now that rabies has reached Denmark, restrictions on the movement of dogs into Germany have been lifted, and Danish exhibitors are frequently seen at shows such as Kiel in North Germany.

SCANDINAVIA
Several good St Bernards have been exhibited in Sweden, and in 1978 a St Bernard was adjudged Best in Show at one of the major exhibitions. The breed is very popular in Sweden as a pet dog, and there is a thriving Breed Club. The breed is also well known in Norway.

HOLLAND
The Dutch St Bernard Club is the second largest in Europe, and the breed has a keen following, although there are few large kennels. The Dutch dogs tend to be smaller and lighter than our British Saints, and have very short muzzles and pronounced stops. One or two British judges have recently been invited to judge in Holland, and have received a warm welcome.

Mrs C. Bradley and Mr P. Hill's Ch. Snowranger Bas V. D. Vrouwenpolder, (1970), imported from Holland.

ISRAEL

St Bernards have recently been introduced into Israel, where a St Bernard Club has been formed. Some early imports came from America, and two from Switzerland, but unfortunately the latter were discovered to be badly affected by hip dysplasia. The desert regions are too hot for the breed, but the cooler mountain area suits them ideally.

SOUTHERN IRELAND

The St Bernard Club of Ireland was founded in 1972 and is now one of the most active Breed Clubs in the country. It holds its annual Championship Show on the first Sunday in July, the normal entry being over 100 dogs including some from the UK. Selective breeding has resulted in a high standard of exhibit, demonstrated by successes at UK shows, including Cruft's.

Irish Champions gain their title by winning a total of forty points or more, which must include at least four major Green Stars (5 points). The value of the Green Star depends entirely on the number of Saints shown on the day, and can never be more than 10 points.

Top winning St Bernard bitch in Ireland in 1985 was Irish Champion Zekeyta Cailin Deas, who gained her title at the age of 20 months. She is one of three champion St Bernards owned by Mr and Mrs A. Long Doyle, and won the Reserve CC at Cruft's in 1987. In 1986 the title of Irish 'Dog of the Year' was won by the St Bernard Irish Champion

American Ch. Esbo V. Grossglockner Von Edelweiss, bred in Germany by Hans Glockner, and owned by Joseph Fleischli.

Burtonswood Black Domino, owned by O. and R. Carey and bred by Miss M. Hindes. Ireland at present has nine living Champion Saints.

America

In the United States, St Bernard registrations have exceeded 35,000 annually, and the breed is among the top ten in popularity. There are numerous St Bernard Clubs in existence, many of them organised on a regional basis. Smooth Saints are much more popular in the States than in this country. St Bernard classes at shows attract enormous entries, and presentation of the dogs is an object lesson, many being professionally handled. American Saints tend to be smaller than those in this country, and much lighter in bone.

The United States St Bernard Standard, based on the International standard, was adopted by the St Bernard Club of America, founded in 1888.

The first American Saints were those exported there from England in the 1880s by the actor J. K. Emmett, who exhibited them on the stage and at fairs. Early breeders concentrated on size rather than type, and many unsound dogs were produced so that interest was lost. One of those to re-awaken interest in the breed during the 1920s was Joseph Fleischli, of the Edelweiss kennels in Springfield, Illinois. He imported stock from Germany and Switzerland, and helped to revive the Breed Club, which had become defunct through lack of support. Another famous early kennel, which supplied the foundation stock of several well-known breeders, was that of Mr and Mrs A. Hayes, who imported from Switzerland to build up their Alpine Plateau strain.

Modern winning kennels in the States are too numerous to mention fully; perhaps the most famous is that of Mrs Beatrice Knight of Oregon, whose Sanctuary Woods Kennel has produced a series of famous Champions, including the noted Ch. Sanctuary Woods Gulliver, a beautiful Smooth.

South Africa

There is great keenness among the small band of St Bernard breeders, who have imported much stock from Britain recently. The geography of the country may often make it necessary for enthusiasts to travel over a thousand miles for show or stud. Cape Town boasts three well-known kennels: R. Blake (Crowhill), Mrs S. Dunlop (Craignish), and Mrs H. Zipp (Oriel). In the Transvaal, well-known breeders are H. Stienen (Arlita), and M. Green (Dinton), while Mrs D. Cartwright (Talisman) keeps the St Bernard to the fore in Natal.

The Far East and Australasia

At the end of the sixties, there was keen demand in Japan for British

Mr and Mrs A. Long Doyle's Irish Champion Zekeyta Cailin Deas. Top winning bitch in Ireland in 1985.

Saints, and several top winners were exported there, as well as many puppies. Owing to disquieting reports about the conditions in Japan, the trade virtually ceased, and there has been little news since. Hong Kong, Malaysia, the Philippines, and New Zealand all have their quota of St Bernard enthusiasts.

St Bernards have been known in Australia for many years. At the Royal Easter Show in New South Wales in 1884 there were seven Saint entries; one was a slut (as bitches were called in those days) owned by August J. Bond, of Sydney, and bred in England from Alp and Queen Bess. At 15 months old she measured 25 in. at shoulder, and weighed 90 lb. During the 1890s, the breed was increasingly popular, and in 1896 there were 41 exhibits and St Bernards were officially registered with the Australian Kennel Club. A prominent breeder at the time was J. P. Claesson, of the Sunlight prefix, who won in 1904 with Ch. Sunlight Snow Queen, whelped in October 1899, bred by Mr Claesson from Sunlight Capstan and Sunlight Lady Beryl. After this time, until the end of the 1930s, entries declined, and separate classes appear to have been discontinued. Until the 1960s, entries seldom exceeded five,

Aust. Ch. Karl of Cornagarth, by Cornagarth Kuno Von Birkenopf ex Ch. Burtonswood Big Time. Bred by M. J. Braysher. Australia's Top Dog of 1977.

but in 1964 Mrs D. Chisman was the first of the modern generation of breeders to import new blood into Australia, bringing about a tremendous renewal of interest.

The top winners line up at Sydney Royal Show in 1978. Challengene Bitch: Merribuff Aosta Adele. Reserve: Zebedee Lady Benem. Challenge Dog: Daneeal Targus. Reserve: Zebedee Sir Baldwin.

Mrs Chisman imported the five-month-old St Rae of Dale End, who had been bred in England by Mrs Read Pearson. His arrival created great publicity and interest. Other imports from the Dale End Kennels followed, including Mrs Chisman's well-known bitch Ch. St. Vanessa of Dale End, who was the first St Bernard to take Reserve Best in Show in Australia. Mrs Chisman has now been granted the Dale End Prefix.

The St Bernard Club of New South Wales was formed in 1976 with forty founder members, and held its first Championship Show in October 1978. Best in show was Ch. Freesea Claudius, owned by Mr and Mrs D. Poisel and bred in Australia from Buta Sir Jeremy and Lindenhall the Joker. Best Bitch went to My Lady Emma, an English export, from Cornagarth Kuno Von Birkenkopf and Cornagarth Anna.

The Victoria St Bernard Club began in 1975, and membership two years later reached 122. It held its first Championship Show in 1977, and 14 Champions paraded at this show. An important recent import

was Ch. Karl of Cornagarth, another son of Cornagath Kuno Von Birkenkopf, imported by Mrs Briggs, of Craigieburn. When mated to Ch. Mummamia Andrea, bred in New South Wales, Karl produced the first St Bernard litter to be reared in Victoria for over twenty years, and registered in Mrs Brigg's prefix, Snowsaint. There are currently 450 St Bernards registered in Victoria.

Although New South Wales and Victoria have the strongest numerical representation of the breed at the moment, the other provinces also have their quota of St Bernard exhibits. In 1978, 35 were registered in Western Australia, where the top winning dog was Burtonswood Be Pert, a son of Ch. Burtonswood Bossy Boots, who has won 57 Challenges, 8 Group Wins, and 3 Best in Shows. Queensland has few registrations, but numbers among its recent winners Ch. Dale End St Angella, bred by Mrs Chisman, who was top winning bitch at Brisbane in 1977. At Adelaide, in South Australia, the top winner is Ch. Snowsaint Champagne C. D., who has group awards to her credit. When mated to Ch. Whaplode Great Expectations, Champagne, who is owned by T. and J. Twigden of the Idyllview prefix, produced the first litter to be registered in South Australia in recent years.

There have been numerous imports recently, and many new bloodlines are now available to Australian breeders. Diversity in quality of the stock sent out from England has resulted in some confusion as to what should be the approved type, and it will be the task of specialist judges to frame the desired type and guide the very keen band of Australian exhibitors. Two bitches sent out recently in whelp from Britain appear to have pointed the way. In 1975 Mrs D. Chisman imported the bitch Cornagarth Chiquita, who won two C. C.s in Britain when owned by Miss Hindes. Her litter to Bossy Boots, born in quarantine, contained two Champions, and a second litter, to a son of Ch. Burtonswood Beloved, numbered five Champions, including the aforementioned Dale End St Angella. Mrs Chisman and her daughter train their Saints in Obedience work, and have had several successes in this sphere.

In 1977 Alpentire Klara Bow was exported in whelp to Ch. Lindenhall Capability Brown, and this mating, of two Smooths, produced some good-quality puppies, including Mrs E. Luke's Merribuff Alps Vontare, who took the Dog Challenge at Melbourne Royal Show in 1978, and Merribuff Aosta Adele, owned by Mrs I. Wallace and Mrs L. Briggs, who took the Bitch Challenge at Sydney Royal in 1978. The Dog Challenge at this show went to Ch. Daneeal Targus, owned by Michael and Sandra Ormsby, a son of Karl of Cornagarth and a bitch imported from America.

Dogs from Britain entering Australia must undergo a three-month quarantine period if travelling by air, or two months if arriving by sea.

There is a quarantine station in each state, and the standard of care is high.

(Information about the St Bernard scene in Australia was kindly supplied by Mrs C. Hodder, Mrs I. Wallace, Mrs D. Chisman, Mrs B Jones and Messrs Ruhen, J. Twigden and P. Fisher.)

New Zealand

Breeding of St Bernards in New Zealand did not begin until well into the twentieth century, although there were occasional imports from 1880 onwards. As interest in the breed in Australia developed during the 1960s, the enthusiasm spread to New Zealand, and there were a number of imports from Great Britain and Australia.

The St Bernard Club of New Zealand was formed in 1979 with Mr R. F. Spellerberg as President. The North Island St Bernard Association was formed that same year. An Australian import Ch. D'Mowbray Star Courage was Best in Show at the North Island's first Open event in 1984.

At present, the New Zealand Kennel Club and the Royal Australian Kennel Club recognise the British Breed Standard, but moves are afoot to persuade these ruling bodies to adopt the International Standard for St Bernards. It seems probable that the new version of the British Standard, will find even less favour with breeders 'down under', widening as it does the gap between the specification for British dogs and the rest of the world.

7 St Bernard Breed Standards

In Britain, the first Standard of Points for St Bernards was drawn up in September 1886 by the Revd Arthur Carter and Mr Frederick Gresham. In June the following year, the International Congress at Zurich drew up another Standard, on which most national standards today are based. In 1986, the English Kennel Club published modified and revised standards for all breeds including the St Bernard. The new version has not, as many hoped, narrowed the gap between the British specification and that used internationally. It was finalised after minimal consultation with the Breed Clubs, and gives little guidance on the finer points which contribute so much to an acceptable type of St Bernard.

The English Standard

(Reproduced by kind permission of the Kennel Club.)

General appearance. Well proportioned and of great substance.

Characteristics. Distinctly marked, large sized mountain rescue dog.

Temperament. Steady, kindly, intelligent, courageous, trustworthy and benevolent.

Head and skull. Large, massive, circumference of skull being rather more than double its length. Muzzle short, full in front of eye, and square at nose end. Cheeks flat, great depth from eye to lower jaw. Lips deep but not too pendulous. From nose to stop perfectly straight and broad. Stop somewhat abrupt and well-defined. Skull broad, slightly rounded at top, with fairly prominent brow. Nose large and black with well-developed nostrils.

Eyes. Of medium size, neither deep set nor prominent, eyelids should be reasonably tight, without any excessive haw. Dark in colour and not staring. There should be no excessive loose wrinkle on brow which would detract from a healthy eye.

Ears. Medium size lying close to cheeks, not heavily feathered.

Mouth. Jaws strong, with a perfect, regular and complete scissor bite, i.e. upper teeth closely overlapping lower teeth and set square to the jaws.

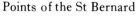

KEY

1. skull 2. occiput 3. ear flap 4. supra-orbital ridge 5. eye 6. stop 7. bridge of muzzle 8. nostril 9. cheek 10. upper flew 11. lower flew 12. dewlap 13. shoulder 14. chest 15. elbow 16. forelimb 17. front pastern 18. foot 19. belly 20. stifle 21. dew-claw 22. hind pastern 23. hind limb 24. hock 25. tail 26. croup 27. loin 28. back 29. withers 30. neck

Points of the St Bernard

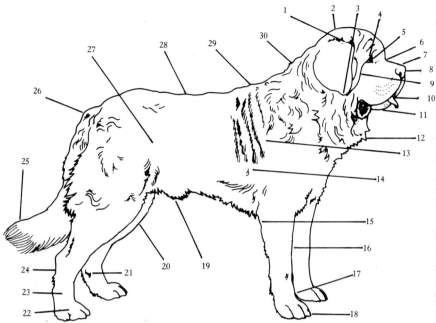

Neck. Long, thick, muscular, slightly arched, dewlap well developed.
Forequarters. Shoulders broad and sloping, well up at withers. Legs straight, strong in bone, of good length.
Body. Back broad, straight, ribs well rounded. Loin wide, very muscular. Chest wide and deep, but never projecting below elbows.
Hindquarters. Legs heavy in bone, hocks well bent, thighs very muscular.
Feet. Large, compact, with well-arched toes. Dewclaws removed.
Tail. Set on rather high, long, carried low when in repose, when excited or in motion should not curl over back.
Gait/Movement. Easy extension, unhurried or smooth, capable of covering difficult terrain.
Coat. In Roughs dense and flat, rather fuller round neck, thighs, and tail well-feathered. In Smooths, close and hound-like, slight feathering on thighs and tail.
Colour. Orange, mahogany-brindle, red-brindle, white with patches on body of any of above-named colours. Markings as follows: White muzzle, white blaze on face, white collar, white chest, white forelegs, feet and end of tail, black shadings on face and ears.
Size. Taller the better provided symmetry is maintained.

Faults. Any departure from the foregoing points should be considered a fault and the seriousness with which the fault should be regarded should be in exact proportion to its degree.

Note. Male animals should have two apparently normal testicles fully descended into the scrotum.

The International Standard

(As adopted by the International Congress at Zurich in 1887.)

THE SHORT-HAIRED ST BERNARD

General character. Powerful, tall, upstanding, with hard muscular development. Massive head and very intelligent expression. In dogs with dark face-markings, the expression is more solemn, but ought never to be bad-tempered.

Head. Like the whole body, very powerful and imposing. The massive skull is wide, slightly arched, and sloping at the sides with a gentle curve into the very well-developed cheek-bones. The occiput is only slightly developed. The supra-orbital ridge is strongly developed, and forms nearly a right angle with the horizontal axis of the head. Between the two supra-orbital arches, and starting at the root of the muzzle, runs a furrow over the whole skull; it is very deep between the supra-orbital arches and strongly defined up the forehead, becoming gradually more shallow towards the base of the occiput. The lines at the sides, from the outer corners of the eyes, diverge considerably towards the back of the head. The skin on the forehead forms somewhat deep wrinkles, more or less distinct, and converging from the supra-orbital arches towards the furrow over the forehead. They are particularly noticeable when the animal is alert, without giving it a savage expression. The stop is clearly defined.

Muzzle. Short, not snipey, and an imaginary line through the muzzle straight down from the stop must be greater than the length of the muzzle. The bridge of the muzzle is straight, not arched, and in some good dogs slightly broken. A rather wide, well marked, shallow furrow runs the whole length of the muzzle from the stop to the nose. The strongly developed lips of the upper jaw do not form an angle at the turning point, but slope with a graceful curve into their lower edge and are slightly over-hanging. The lips of the lower jaw must not be pendant. Teeth in proportion to the size of the head are only moderately large. A black roof to the mouth is preferred.

Nose. Very substantial and broad, with well-dilated nostrils, and like the lips always black.

Ears. Medium-sized, with the burr strongly developed, which causes them to stand away slightly at the base and, bending suddenly, they drop without any curl close to the side of the head. The flaps are not too leathery, and form rounded triangles slightly elongated towards the points. The front edge ought to lie close to the head, but the back edge may stand away a little, particularly when the dog is at attention. Ears with weak burr, causing them to lie close to the head from their roots, give it an oval shape, which imparts too much softness to the outline, whereas strongly developed ear-muscles make the skull appear more angular and wider, thus giving the head more character.

Eyes. Set more to the front than the sides, are of moderate size, brown or nut-brown, with an intelligent and friendly expression, set moderately deep. The lower eyelids do not, as a rule, fit close to the eyeballs, and form towards the inner corner an angular wrinkle. Eyelids which are too pendant, with conspicuously protruding lachrymal glands, or a very red haw, are objectionable.

Neck. Set on high, and carried upright when the animal is animated, otherwise horizontal or slightly downward. The junction between head and neck distinctly indicated. The neck is very muscular, and rounded at the sides, giving it the appearance of shortness. The dewlap should be clearly noticeable, but too great development of this is not desirable.

Shoulders. Sloping and broad, very muscular and powerful, and well-developed at the withers.

Chest. Well rounded and moderately deep. It must not reach to below the elbows.

Back. Very broad, and only slightly arched over the loins. Otherwise straight to the haunches, and from the haunches gently sloping to the rump, it merges gradually into the tail.

Hind-quarters. Well developed; legs very muscular.

Belly. Only slightly drawn up, and showing distinctly where it joins the very powerful region of the kidneys.

Tail. Starting broad and powerful, directly from the rump, is long, very heavy, ending in a blunt tip. In repose it hangs straight down, turning gently upwards in the lower third. In many specimens the point is slightly turned up, and hangs, therefore, in the shape of an 'f'; in excitement, all dogs carry their tails more or less raised, but it must not go to the extent of being erect, or even curled over the back; a slight curling round of the tip is sooner admissible.

Forelegs. Straight, strong, very powerful and heavily muscled.

Hind legs. Have moderately angulated hocks. The presence of dewclaws is not desirable.

Feet. Broad, with strong toes, moderately well closed up, and rather high knuckles. The so-called dew-claws (Wolfklauen) which sometimes occur on the inside of the hind legs are imperfectly developed toes; they are of no use to the dog and are not taken into consideration when judging.

Coat. Very dense, broken-haired, lying smooth, hard, without being rough to the touch. Thighs are slightly feathered. The hair at the root of the tail is rather long and dense, getting gradually shorter towards the point. The tail appears bushy, but not feathered.

Colour. White with red, or red with white, the red in all its various shades; white with light to dark-barred brindle patches, or these colours with white markings. The colours red, brindle, and tawny, are of equal value. Obligatory markings are white chest, feet, point of tail, and white round the nose and collar. The white spot on the nape of the neck, and a blaze are much desired. Never self-coloured, or without any white. All other colours are faulty, except the favourite dark shadings in the face markings, and on the ears.

Height at shoulder. Dogs (measured with the Hound measure) ought to be not less than 70 cm, and bitches 65 cm (27½ and 26½ in). The bitches are throughout of a less powerful and slighter build than the dogs.

Faults. As faulty, are to be considered all variations not in accordance with these points, such as sway back, disproportionately long back, hocks too much bent, or spaces between the toes, with upward growing hair.

THE LONG-HAIRED (ROUGH) ST BERNARD

The long-haired dog is exactly like the other, with the exception of the coat. This should never be broken-haired, but of medium length, flat or slightly wavy, but never very wavy, curly, or shaggy. The coat is, as a rule, more wavy on the back, particularly in the region of the hip and rump. The tail is bushy, well covered with moderately long hair. Wavy or locky hair on the tail is not desirable. A flagged tail or one with a parting is faulty. The face and ears are covered with short, soft hair; at the base of the ears longer silky hair is permissible, in fact this is nearly always the case. The feather on the forelegs is only slight, but on the thighs it appears bushy.

The American Standard

(Based on the International Standard and approved by the American Kennel Club in May 1959.)

General. Powerful, proportionately tall figure, strong and muscular in every part, with powerful head and most intelligent expression. In dogs with a dark mask the expression appears more stern, but never ill-natured.

Head. Like the whole body, very powerful and imposing. The massive skull is wide, slightly arched, and the sides slope in a gentle curve into the very strongly developed, high cheek bones. Occiput only moderately developed. The supra-orbital ridge is very strongly developed and forms nearly a right angle with the horizontal axis of the head. Deeply embedded between the eyes and starting at the root of the muzzle, a furrow runs over the whole skull. It is strongly marked in the first half, gradually disappearing towards the base of the occiput. The lines at the side of the head diverge considerably from the outer corner of the eyes towards the back of the head. The skin of the forehead, above the eyes, forms rather noticeable wrinkles, more or less pronounced, which converge towards the furrow. Especially when the dog is in action, the wrinkles are more visible, without in the least giving the impression of morosity. Too strongly developed wrinkles are not desired. The slope from the skull to the muzzle is sudden and rather steep.

The muzzle is short, does not taper, and the vertical depth at the root of the muzzle must be greater than the length of the muzzle. The bridge of the muzzle is not arched, but straight; in some dogs, occasionally, slightly broken. A rather wide, well-marked, shallow furrow runs from the root of the muzzle over the entire bridge of the muzzle to the nose. The flews of the upper jaw are strongly developed, not sharply cut, but hanging in a beautiful curve into the lower edge, and slightly overhanging. The flews of the lower jaw must not be deeply pendant. The teeth should be sound and strong and should meet in either a scissors or an even bite, the scissors bite being preferable. The undershot bite, although sometimes found in good specimens, is not desirable. The overshot bite is a fault. A black roof to the mouth is desirable.

Nose. (Schwamm) Very substantial, broad, with wide open nostrils, and like the lips, always black.

Ears. Of medium size, rather high set, with very strongly developed burr (Muschel) at the base. They stand slightly away from the head at the base, then drop with a sharp bend to the side and cling to the head without a turn. The flap is tender and forms a rounded triangle, slightly elongated towards the point, the front edge lying firmly to the head, whereas the back edge may stand somewhat away from the head, especially when the dog is at attention. Lightly set ears, which at the base immediately cling to the head, give it an oval and too little marked exterior, whereas a strongly developed base gives the skull a squarer, broader and much more expressive appearance.

Eyes. Set more to the front than the sides, are of medium size, dark brown, with intelligent, friendly expression, set moderately deep. The lower eyelids, as a rule, do not close completely and, if that is the case, form an angular wrinkle towards the inner corner of the eye. Eyelids which are too deeply pendant and show conspicuously the lachrymal glands, or a very red haw, and eyes that are too light, are objectionable.

Neck. Set high, very strong and in action is carried erect. Otherwise horizontally or slightly downward. The junction of head and neck is distinctly marked by an indentation. The nape of the neck is very muscular and rounded at the sides which makes the neck appear rather short. The dewlap of throat and neck is well-pronounced: too strong development, however, is not desirable.

Shoulders. Sloping and broad, very muscular and powerful. The withers are strongly pronounced.

Chest. Very well arched, moderately deep, not reaching below the elbows.

Back. Very broad, perfectly straight as far as the haunches, from there gently sloping to the rump, and merging imperceptibly into the root of the tail.

Hind-quarters. Well-developed. Legs very muscular.

Belly. Distinctly set off from the very powerful loin section, only little drawn up.

Tail. Starting broad and powerful, directly from the rump is long, very heavy, ending in a powerful tip. In repose it hangs straight down, turning upward in the lower third only, which is not considered a fault. In a great many specimens the tail is carried with the edge slightly bent and therefore hangs down in the shape of an 'f'. In action, all dogs carry the tail more or less turned upward. However, it may not be carried too erect or by any means rolled over the back. A slight curling of the tip is sooner admissible.

Forearms. Very powerful and extraordinarily muscular.

Forelegs. Straight, strong.

Hind legs. Hocks of moderate angulation. Dew-claws are not desired. If present, they must not obstruct gait.

Feet. Broad, with strong toes, moderately closed, and with rather high knuckles. The so-called dew-claws which sometimes occur on the inside of the hind legs are imperfectly developed toes. They are no use to the dog and are not taken into consideration in judging. They may be removed by surgery.

Coat. Very dense, short-haired (stockhaarig), lying smooth, tough, without however feeling rough to the touch. The thighs are slightly bushy. The tail at the root has longer and denser hair which gradually becomes shorter towards the tip. The tail appears bushy, not forming a flag.

Colour. White with red or red with white, the red in its various shades; brindle patches with white markings. The colours red and brown–yellow are of entirely equal value. Necessary markings are: white chest, feet and tip of tail, nose band, collar or spot on the nape; the latter and blaze are very desirable. Never of one colour or without white. Faulty are all other colours, except the favourite dark shadings on the head (mask) and ears. One distinguishes between mantle dogs and splash coated dogs.

Height at shoulder. Dogs should be 27½ in. minimum, bitches 25½ in. Female animals are of finer and more delicate build.

Considered as faults are all deviations from the standard, as for instance a sway back and a disproportionately long back, hocks too much bent, straight hind-quarters, upward growing hair in spaces between the toes, out at elbows, cow hocks, and weak pasterns.

LONG-HAIRED

The long-haired type completely resembles the short-haired type except for the coat, which is not short-haired (stockhaarig), but of medium length plain to slightly wavy, never rolled or curly, and not shaggy either. Usually, on the back, especially from the region of the haunches to the rump, the hair is more wavy, a condition, by the way, that is slightly indicated in the short-haired dogs. The tail is bushy with dense hair of moderate length. Rolled or curly hair on the tail is not desirable. A tail with parted hair, or a flag tail, is faulty. Face and ears are covered with short and soft hair; longer hair at the base of the ear is permissible. Forelegs only slightly feathered; thighs very bushy.

The variety of type seen in winning Saints in Britain, America, and on the Continent is evidence that Breed Standards allow much flexibility of interpretation. Dogs in this country are criticised abroad for being too dark in mask, and for the prevalence of ticking (dark or brownish spotting) on white areas of legs and muzzle. They are also said to show too much eye haw. English breeders dislike the more prominent, rounded eyes which are often seen in the Continental dogs, and the prevalent cheek bumps, which are not listed as faults in the International Standard.

These are minor points of difference, and all Standards make it abundantly clear that breeders must aim for a massive, powerful, heavily boned dog, with a beautiful expression of intelligent benevolence. Above all, the temperament must match the essential expression, for if benignity is missing, however closely the dog fits the standard, he cannot truly be called a 'Saint'.

'Massive' does not only mean tall, although this is important. The true St Bernard is heavily boned, with powerful, muscular shoulders, strong loins and hind-quarters, and a large imposing head. It should be emphasised that a massive dog is a powerful dog, not a fat one! The minimum heights called for in the International Standard are exceeded today by most St Bernards in show rings throughout the world, and the requirement of the English Standard 'the taller the better, provided

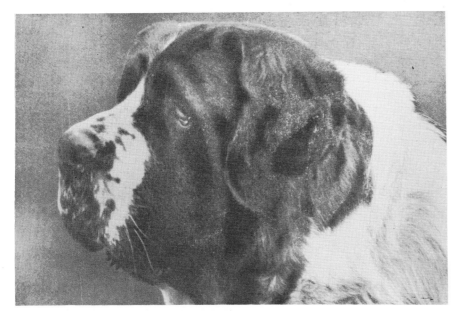

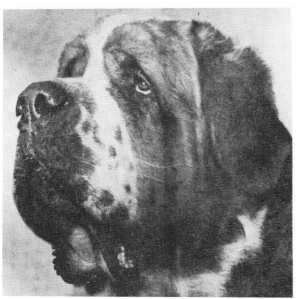

Left: Mrs K. Staines's Ch. Abbotspass Benedick. This dog was noted for its benevolent expression, but was sadly lacking in 'stop'.

Below Left: An example of a St Bernard with the correct 'stop', Mrs D. Ayckbourne's Daphnydene Laertes.

Below Right: This 1936 head study of Mrs M. Wood's Ch. Copleydene St Goliath shows the squareness and depth of muzzle so desirable in the breed.

that symmetry is maintained', is an excellent yardstick when judging. Power, type and soundness, are of greater importance than height, but if you have these attributes in a dog of great and imposing stature, then you have a truly great St Bernard.

The head properties of a St Bernard are so important that, under the old points system, now obsolete, 40% of the total marks were allocated to the head. To assess a St Bernard fairly, one must understand and appreciate the correct head structure. The skull must be well-rounded from front to back, and must look broad and slightly rounded at the top when viewed from the front. English dogs before the World War II were criticised for flatness of skull, no doubt a legacy of the Mastiff cross, which tended to make the expression stern and hard. A clearly defined stop is of the utmost importance, and should be a true right angle, not a mere slope; many present-day dogs fail in this respect.

The muzzle should be broad and flat across the top, in fact, the wider and deeper the better. Its measurement in a downward direction, at the point where it leaves the stop, should be at least as great as its

St Bernard Heads

1
The ideal head, showing correct stop; rounded skull; short, deep muzzle; well-rounded flews; small diamond eye.

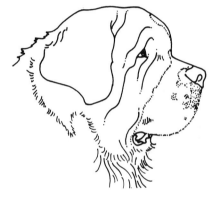

2
This dog has a good short muzzle and correctly rounded flews, but its head is spoiled by lack of roundness in top-skull.

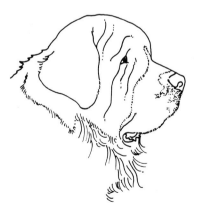

3
This dog has a good round skull, but its muzzle is too long and sloping, and the flews are too 'cut away'.

length from stop to nostril. The flatness across the top of the muzzle is most essential; it must never be convex, or tented. The shallow furrow running along the upper surface of the muzzle will be absent if the top of the muzzle is not flat. Although the muzzle must be short in relation to its depth, it must not be too short; the ultra-short muzzles favoured by certain breeders in the past certainly imparted an impression of width and depth, but were invariably accompanied by deterioration in soundness, and lack of correct physical balance.

The sides of the muzzle must not only be deep and flat, but the lower front corners of the upper flews should be generously rounded. The lower flews should not be too pendulous, or the dog will tend to slaver copiously; rows of drooling St Bernards on the show benches are not a good advertisement for the breed!

Breed standards differ in their definition of the correct St Bernard bite. The British standard used to call for a level mouth, listing over- and undershot jaws as faults. The Kennel Club now insists that only the scissor bite is correct, and the revised standard clearly demands this. Pincer bites (level), are still, under the revised standards, tolerated in Newfoundlands and Pyreneans, but not, in St Bernards, which is unfortunate, as a strongly developed lower jaw gives the desired

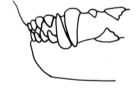

(1) *Scissor bite* (demanded in new British Standard and preferable according to American Standard)

(2) *Level bite* (tolerated under American Standard but not under new British Standard)

(3) *Undershot bite* (often overlooked by judges, as it gives strength to lower jaw)

(4) *Overshot bite* (should never be overlooked)

squareness and strength to the muzzle. The American Standard speci-
fies a scissor or a level bite, the scissor being preferable. The International Standard makes no mention of the correct bite, and an
undershot jaw is often regarded as acceptable, provided the lower
incisors are not visible when the mouth is closed.

The facial expression of many Saints today is ruined by faulty eyes.
These should be as dark as possible and the iris should look almost as
dark as the pupil. Light, staring eyes are one of the most serious faults
possible. In view of the prevalence in the breed of entropion (in-turned
eyelids) and ectropion (turned-out eyelids), the eye specification in the
new British Standard has been drastically revised, and the 'deep set'
eye which used to be the norm, and contributed to the St Bernard's
kindly and wise expression, is no longer required. It used to be said
that the previous standard encouraged the breeding of dogs with patho-
logically unsound eyes, having either faulty eyelids or showing excess-

The author's Ch.
Lindenhall High
Commander. The
width of the facial
blaze detracts from
the expression.

ive haw, and the changes in the standard were designed to prevent this. The new standard implies that excessive skin folds above the eyes must be avoided as they may detract from a healthy eye. This is only partly true, as it is not so much the excessive skin which causes the problem, but rather the insufficient development of the bony ridge above the eye, known as the supra orbital ridge, which fails to prevent loose skin from falling forward over the eye. In the past it has been possible to breed St Bernards with a slight wrinkle, or 'diamond' towards the inner corner of the eye, and yet retain a healthy eye, and it will be unfortunate if the change in our standard means that we eventually lose the traditional St Bernard expression.

The ear-set should be slightly oblique, and not too high or low. The back edges of the ear flaps should stand slightly away from the head, thereby accentuating the broad and rounded appearance of the skull when viewed from the front.

The English Standard calls for a lengthy, thick, muscular, and slightly arched neck – in other words, for a neck like that of a shire horse. The muscularity and strength of the neck may give it the impression of being of only moderate length, and in rough-coated dogs this impression is accentuated by the profusion of the coat in the neck region. The neck must never be so short and broad as to give the appearance that the head is growing out of the shoulders. A generous dewlap is desirable, accentuating the impression of power in the front, but it must not be so well-developed that, when viewed from the side, the dog has an unbalanced appearance.

The chest must be broad, with well-sprung ribs and plenty of heart room. It should be moderately deep but must never reach below the elbows. Many Saints with this fault also dip in back, which gives the impression that the body is slung between the two limb girdles. An insufficiently deep, or too narrow, chest is also undesirable, and gives the dog a shelly appearance and lack of power. Good lay-back of shoulders is essential.

St Bernard Fronts

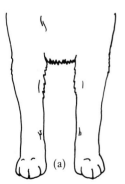

Good front, with straight legs and tight cat feet

(a)

Chest too narrow, elbows under body & feet turned out

(b)

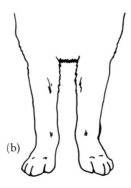

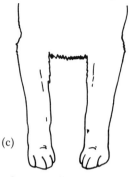

(c)

Out at elbows with
feet turning inwards

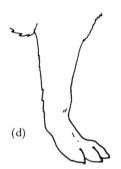

(d)

Side view of weak
pasterns and splay
foot.

The front legs should be very strongly boned, again giving the appearance of power, and should be of good length. They should be straight and vertical from the elbow to the feet, with strong pasterns. Many St Bernards today are sabre-legged, that is to say the front legs are bowed backwards, which is not correct.

The St Bernard should have a broad, level back, on which one could stand a tea tray! The back should slope slightly downwards at the croup to the set-on of the tail. If the tail is set too high there will be no downward slope, and the back will appear too long. A male St Bernard should be fairly short-coupled, but more length is acceptable in a bitch. The loins must be very thick and powerful, and the belly must never appear tucked-up.

The hind-quarters are most important, and should be large with moderately well-turned stifles. The hocks must be set low, and only a very slight turning out of the back feet is permissible. Cow hocks and straight stifles are common faults in this breed, as are loose hocks, which owing to a shortness of the calcaneal process, may result in an almost double-jointed action when the dog moves. Owing to the weight of the body, an over-angulated St Bernard is most undesirable.

When a Saint moves, his hocks should not turn in or out, but should move straight forward in a vertical direction. The feet should not drag, nor should they be lifted higher than necessary. If a dog is straight in the stifle, he will tend to swing his hocks in an outward direction when moving, in order to gain propulsion. The front feet should also clear the ground without dragging, but a high-stepping, hackney action is incorrect. They, too, should move in a straight vertical plane, neither swinging out like paddles, nor crossing inwards, and plaiting.

A St Bernard's feet must be broad and tight, with powerful, strongly-arched toes. They should be like those of a cat, rather than

St Bernard Hind-
quarters

(1)

Good hind-quarters with
well-turned stifles,
slightly bent hocks, and
cat feet.

(2)

Faulty hind-quarters the
croup is too sloping, and
the dog is cow-hocked,
with splayed hind feet.

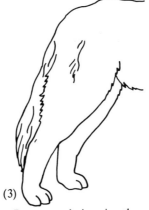

(3)

Poor angulation in the
hind-quarters. The
stifles are straight and
there is little turn in the
hocks.

(4)

Good hind-quarters.

(5)

Cow hocks, with hind
feet outward and too far
apart.

flat, splay-toed, and hare-like. Splay feet are a common fault, and can
sometimes be improved by exercise on hard ground.

In the rough-coated dog, the tail is one of the most beautiful
features, and the coat on it should be long and profuse. As explained in
the International Standard, a slight curl in the tail tip is permissible,
but a ring tail is a fault, and in the smooth-coated variety, a very
obvious one. The height of the tail set will govern the tail carriage: if
the tail is set too high, the tail will never hang down properly, but will

A St Bernard
showing obvious
faults: snipey
muzzle, too cut
away in flew, flat
skull, too short in
neck, high tail-set,
lack of slope in
croup, and very
straight stifles.

An expressive
Smooth, head, with
correct side folds
and deep, well-
rounded flews: A. K.
Gaunt's Cornagarth
Gulliver, (1950).

be carried gaily or curled over the back when the animal moves.

The ideal markings are described in the Standard, but less attention is paid to them in this country than overseas. A dog with copy-book markings is less difficult to breed than one of good type and conformation, and in our opinion the latter should always be paramount.

8 Selective Breeding

Breeding and rearing a litter of St Bernards is a time-consuming and costly undertaking, which should not be embarked upon without the most careful consideration. With a bitch of any breed the novice breeder can encounter unforeseen problems, but with St Bernards these may be greatly magnified. The initial stud fee may be high; there may be whelping problems, with resultant large veterinary bills; it is not uncommon for a heavy bitch to overlay several puppies, and a good litter may be much reduced in consequence. Lastly, rearing costs are considerable, as to give the puppies the best start in life, a liberal diet of high quality food is essential. All this makes it necessary for high prices to be asked for the puppies, and they do not always command a ready market. These are all points which should receive much thought before you decide to breed a litter of St Bernards.

There can be few greater satisfactions than winning in the show ring with stock of one's own breeding. If one is planning to breed with the aim of producing show-quality offspring, and possibly of laying the foundations of a winning show strain, some attention must be paid to the principles of selective breeding. Although luck does play a part in all livestock breeding, and a good puppy may occasionally result from the haphazard mating of two individuals, the best results are always achieved when the parents are chosen for their individual merits and the compatibility of their bloodlines. It is often said that breeding is an art, not a science, this is true up to a point, but only by understanding something of the laws of inheritance and proven methods of successful breeding can one make a carefully considered choice of foundation stock.

There are many excellent books available on the science of genetics and its application to the breeding of dogs, but the following outline of the principles of inheritance may be helpful to novice breeders. It is fairly widely known that the physical make-up of any living organism is determined by hereditary factors, known as genes, which are carried on structures called chromosomes, present in the nuclei of every cell in the body. These chromosomes occur in pairs; the dog has 39 pairs, bearing a total of some 150,000 genes. When the reproductive cells are formed in the testes and ovaries of the parent animals, each pair of chromosomes separates, so that the sperm and the egg only contain half the normal quota of chromosomes. When they unite at the moment of fertilisation, each contributes half the total chromosome content of the cells of the new individual. In this way each parent makes an equal contribution to the gene pattern of the offspring. This pattern can vary considerably in all the different members of a litter, as it is a matter of chance which one of any pair of parental genes may be present in the make-up of any individual puppy.

Each gene is specific in action; one pair may help to govern eye colour, another size, another coat-type etc. When each one of a pair of genes influences an opposing factor, such as light or dark eye colour, the influence of one must over-ride that of the other. The gene having the stronger effect is said to be dominant, and the weaker gene is known as recessive. In certain cases the genes may exert equal opposing influences, so that in the offspring a certain factor may be present to a degree intermediate between two extremes.

If a puppy inherits a dominant gene from one parent and a recessive from the other, it will manifest the physical feature controlled by the dominant gene, but, when used for breeding, it may pass the recessive gene to its offspring. Should a puppy inherit similar recessive genes from both its parents, the character, possibly undesirable, brought about by these genes will be manifested, as there will be no dominant gene present to counteract them. Thus, for example, two dark-eyed dogs, each carrying the recessive gene for light eye colour, can produce a light-eyed puppy. It follows from this that, before planning a litter, one must learn as much as possible about the forebears listed in the pedigrees of the prospective parents. Ideally. one should know each dog, and carry a picture of it in one's mind, so that its faults as well as its virtues can be taken into consideration. These undesirable features, although not apparent perhaps in the immediate ancestors, may be inherited as recessive genes from individuals further back in the pedigree.

The aim of breeding must always be to fix good points and breed out bad ones. Indiscriminate and haphazard breeding may do great harm to the breed, as there is always the possibility that, by doubling up on hidden recessive genes, undesirable faults will be brought to light. In order to 'fix' a type, and ultimately to establish a pure strain, experienced breeders must employ inbreeding and line breeding methods, so an explanation of these terms is relevant.

Inbreeding
Inbreeding is the mating together of very closely related parents; matings of brother to sister, father to daughter, mother to son, or half-brother to sister, are all covered by this term. This type of breeding does not cause defects, but by increasing the probability of

doubling up on any recessive genes carried by both parents, inbreeding is likely to make recessive faults apparent. By rejecting any stock manifesting these undesirable defects, a breeder can rid his strain from these faults, and ultimately be left with pure stock. Only by ruthless culling of imperfect stock can benefit be gained from this method of close breeding. It is essential to know exactly what lies behind animals intended for inbreeding, and the parents must obviously carry as few apparent faults as possible. Inbreeding from outstanding animals can produce exceptionally good stock, but if the parents are bad, the offspring will be even worse. Prolonged inbreeding within a strain can cause loss of size and vigour, and may result in offspring of unsound temperament. A novice breeder, tempted to try inbreeding methods, must not only have confidence in the excellence of the stock it is proposed to use, but carefully consider the risks involved, and the implications of ruthless culling.

Line breeding

Line breeding is more widely practised than inbreeding. It is a slower method of establishing a distinctive strain, but, because it entails less culling of defective stock, it has more to recommend it from the novice's point of view. Line breeding includes such crosses as grandfather to grand-daughter, grandmother to grandson, and cousin to cousin. The term line breeding is used loosely to cover the breeding back to an outstanding dog in the pedigree of one's bitch, or to his close relatives such as brothers and sons, which it is hoped carry a similar gene make-up. Line breeding in this way to a dog of one's ideal type will result in a preponderance of that dog's virtues (and faults) in one's stock. An inbred or closely line-bred stud dog will usually be more dominant than one resulting from more distant breeding, as he should carry a more uniform gene make-up.

Out-crossing

All breeders must occasionally introduce new blood into their strains to increase size and vigour, but any such out-cross mating must be planned with great care. The true out-cross is a union of completely unrelated animals, with no common ancestry. The existing St Bernard bloodlines in this country are considerably inbred, and suitable out-crosses are difficult to obtain. In the past, occasional introduction of Continental Saints has been made to provide new blood, as in the case of Mrs R. L. Walker's Ch. Peldartor Anka Von der Ducke Schleuse, who was imported from Germany. In her litter by Ch. Peldartor Charnwood Bruno, Anka bred Ch. Peldartor Ranee, and Ch. Peldartor Rosseau, who in his turn sired Ch. Cornagarth Master of Durrowabbey. A daughter of Master, Ch. Cornagarth True Love, was the dam of Ch. Cornagarth Burtonswood Princess, whose titled offspring included Ch. Cornagarth Stroller, Ch. Cornagarth He's Grand, and Ch. Cornagarth Shanta.

The selected out-cross should always be as distant as possible, so that the doubling up of recessive faults that may be shared by common ancestors is avoided. Out-crossing always carries an inherent risk of introducing new undesirable traits into a strain. The puppies resulting from an out-cross mating are almost invariably of assorted type, and a breeder will naturally select from them those which most closely resemble his own line and prefered type. By mating these back to individuals of his own strain, the benefit of the out-cross often becomes apparent in the second and third generation. Normally, a stud dog resulting from an out-cross is less dominant than one more closely bred.

The brevity of the English Standard for St Bernards permits a wide variety of interpretation as to which is the correct type. During the heyday of the Cornagarth Kennels, most judges favoured Mr Gaunt's taste in type, and it became accepted as the only correct one. In breeding one should, we feel, try to keep a wide outlook and recognise the merits in types other than one's own, provided these are within the Standard.

Miss P. M. Muggleton's German import Ch. Pankraz Von Den Drei Helmen of Bernmont, born 1982, currently being used as an outcross.

9 Breeding Stock, Mating and Whelping

THE BROOD BITCH

If you have finally decided that you have the facilities, time and money to breed your first litter of St Bernards, perhaps as a step towards establishing a successful show kennel, the choice of a suitable mother will be of paramount importance. The bitch you chose must be of good type, sound, well-balanced, broad in body, and, above all, the possessor of a kind and steady temperament. A poor type of bitch is unlikely to breed good puppies, so it is essential to choose a mother without serious hereditary faults. Occasionally, a mediocre bitch can throw a 'flyer', but this can be a disadvantage to the breed, as her descendants in subsequent generations may well inherit her faults. If the bitch from which you plan to breed does not measure up to these exacting requirements, it may be as well to keep her as a pet, and to try to buy one more suitable.

Good young breeding bitches are difficult to purchase, and, if available, the value of their potential litters will make their cost prohibitive. If you are offered a young bitch who has already been used for breeding, it pays to approach the deal with caution, and to make tactful enquiries about her mothering and whelping capabilities. Do not be tempted to purchase an old bitch, who has already had several litters, as after the third litter the number and quality of a bitch's puppies frequently declines. Occasionally, a breeder may sell a bitch on whole or part breeding terms, retaining the ownership of some of its future offspring, but arrangements like this often mean that you must relinquish the best puppies in the first and sometimes the second litter. If entering into an arrangement of this sort, always make sure that the conditions are clearly set out and signed in a written agreement, as misunderstandings can so easily arise.

If it is not possible to purchase a bitch of breeding age, it will be necessary to be more patient, and buy a suitable puppy. Try to choose one from a winning strain, and a family of good whelpers, and hope that, with careful rearing, she will make the grade. Many faults apparent in adult St Bernards are not detectable at the puppy stage, but an honest breeder, careful of the reputation of his kennel, should help you to select a puppy without obvious imperfections, and showing promise of show potential. Very short-coupled bitches seldom make

Miss M. Hindes's Smooth Ch. Burtonswood Beloved. Dam of six Champions including the celebrated Ch. Burtonswood Bossy Boots.

good broods, as ample length of loin, that may be a handicap in the show ring, is an asset in a breeding animal.

A bitch to be used for breeding must be in tip-top physical condition, which will be achieved by good feeding and adequate exercise. She should be free from worms, and must not be carrying excess fat. It is a good plan to supply her with extra vitamins during the period prior to the anticipated mating, and cod-liver oil and wheat-germ oil are beneficial if given in moderation.

THE STUD DOG

The choice of a suitable stud dog must be made well in advance, and requires considerable care and thought. Although there is an old saying that 'the strength of a kennel lies in its bitches', the dog plays an equally important role.

The need to line up the pedigree of the dog with that of the bitch has been explained in the preceding chapter, and it is probably wise for a novice to line breed in the first instance. It is most important before reaching a final decision to visit one of the large championship shows in order to study winning dogs and their progeny. The biggest winners do not always make the best sires, although, because they are well-known names in the show-ring, their services may be widely used, and from their numerous litters the occasional good offspring will probably arise. When assessing a dog's progeny, one should always take into consideration the quality of the bitches he has been fortunate, or unfortunate, enough to mate.

You should always have confidence in your own judgement, and preference for type. Other breeders may condemn a dog because he belongs to a rival kennel, but if you like him, his pedigree lines up, and he comes close to matching your picture of the ideal St Bernard, you should not be afraid to use him. After all, it is his type you hope to stamp on your future kennel!

One should not be deterred from using the dog of one's choice because a long journey is involved in taking the bitch to his kennels. Do however gain assurance beforehand that the dog is experienced, and has the right instincts; nothing is more annoying than travelling several hundreds of miles with a bitch at the height of her season, only to find a shy stud dog, or an owner who does not know how to conduct a mating between two St Bernards.

It is wise to ascertain the amount of the stud fee before finally arranging the mating, but its cost should be immaterial, if the dog is the best choice for your bitch. If costs are a matter of prime consideration, it is better not to attempt to breed St Bernards. The high fee charged for a leading sire should in any case be compensated by the high value of his puppies. Some breeders are prepared to accept one, or sometimes two, puppies in lieu of a stud fee, but any arrangement of this nature should be very precise, and should specify who has first pick of the litter. If you are breeding with the aim of producing a good show specimen for yourself, it is somewhat galling to see the only outstanding puppy in your first litter whisked off to the kennels of the stud-dog owner! On the other hand, should no puppies result from the mating, you will not have lost financially by paying a high fee without result.

Some novice breeders are keen to keep their own stud dog, but this is unwise unless the dog is of outstanding quality and likely to suit the bitches from which it is proposed to breed. If a dog is primarily a house pet and companion, he may not in any case make a keen stud, and his use for this purpose can result in him becoming restless and embarassingly amorous in the future. It is more satisfactory to build up a good bitch line by the use of other peoples' stud dogs, and later, when an outstanding dog puppy is bred, to keep it.

Temperament in the chosen stud dog is of prime importance, and should be of the nature you wish to stamp on the puppies. However suitable in other respects, if the dog fails in this factor, he should not be used. A good stud dog should be masculine and assertive, but never bad-tempered. He must always show to a marked degree the essential qualities of power and good head type, and like the brood bitch, he should be in the best possible physical condition.

THE BITCH'S SEASON
The age of a bitch's first season can vary from six to over twelve months, but it normally occurs when she is about nine months old, and, after this, should be repeated about every six months. Opinions vary about the most suitable age to mate a St Bernard, some breeders believing that a bitch should not be bred from until she is at least two and has completed her physical development. We have had the best results from mating for the first time at about fourteen to eighteen months, usually during the second season, and by doing so have avoided the whelping difficulties often met with in older bitches.

Signs of an approaching heat (oestrum) are a swelling of the vulva, accompanied first by a mucus discharge. The bitch will be inclined to urinate more frequently, and will begin to flirt with dogs and with other bitches. When the season begins, the vulva will become more swollen and hard, and the discharge will become bloody. As the time for mating approaches, the vulva will become soft and relaxed, and the discharge may lose its colour, although some bitches continue to show blood until the season ends. Bitches vary from one another as to when they are ready to be mated, but this point is usually reached about twelve or thirteen days after the commencement of the red discharge. Until the eggs of the bitch have left the ovaries and descended into the Fallopian tubes to await fertilisation by the male sperm, it is useless to take the bitch to the dog, as she will be infertile. Many stud dogs have been unfairly blamed for unproductive matings, when in actual fact the fault has lain with the over-anxious owner of the bitch who has brought the animal for service too early in the season. When a bitch is 'ready' she will often curl her tail sideways if the vulva is stimulated, and if a clean and well-Vaselined forefinger is inserted into the genital passage, it should penetrate easily without obstruction.

The owner of the stud dog should always be contacted as soon as the bitch's season commences so that a provisional date for the mating can be arranged. Final arrangements cannot actually be made until the bitch is ready, as one never knows quite when this will be. In this matter you must suit the bitch's convenience rather than your own, if you wish your journey to be fruitful. The number of bitches ready on Sundays always amazes us, but then they are Saints!

MATING

It is usual for the bitch to be taken to the stud dog's kennels, rather than vice versa, and she should be given the opportunity to empty her bladder on arrival. A smear of Vaseline (not a plug) inserted with a clean finger inside the vagina will lubricate the passage for the insertion of the penis. A maiden bitch may exhibit signs of nervousness, in which case a preliminary romp with the dog may help to relax her. If the bitch is ready and receptive, and the stud dog up to his job, the mating should not prove difficult. Most stud-dog owners expect the person bringing the bitch to be able to hold her firmly while the dog is mounting and penetrating. Once the base of the penis has swollen up inside the bitch, it cannot be withdrawn, and the pair are then said to be 'tied'. After a few minutes to allow for maximum swelling, the dog can be turned so that he is standing on all fours, back to back with the bitch, which is the most comfortable position for both partners. A 'tie' usually lasts about half an hour, until the swelling on the penis has subsided and the dog can withdraw it. The dog should be allowed to lick the bitch's rear after the mating, as this makes the bitch contract her passage, and retain the sperm. She should then be removed and put somewhere to rest quietly before the journey home. The stud-dog owner should make sure the dog is fully retracted before returning him to his kennel.

It should be mentioned here that some stud dogs never achieve a tie, and yet beget puppies, but most breeders consider that a tie is essential to a satisfactory mating. If there is no tie, or if the bitch's season intensifies during the days following the mating, some stud dog owners will give a second service, but normally this is not necessary, and can result in a protracted whelping. Due to nervousness, it is sometimes difficult to achieve a satisfactory mating for a maiden bitch, and, in this case, it is advisable to mate a second time, when she will often be more relaxed.

Very occasionally one may encounter breeders who believe in allowing the dog and bitch to mate naturally without assistance, and sometimes without supervision. This is not a method to be recommended for St Bernards, as there is risk of injury to the bitch, who may be unable to support the dog's heavy weight. The dog, if allowed to wear himself out by fruitless attempts at penetration, may become exhausted or suffer rupture or other injury.

If a stud fee is being paid, it should be handed to the breeder after the mating has taken place. The bitch's owner should receive a receipt, containing the date of birth on which the puppies are due, and a copy of the stud dog's pedigree. Most owners agree to give a free service during the next season, if the mating is unproductive, but this should not be taken for granted.

CARE OF THE BITCH DURING PREGNANCY

It is most important not to let your bitch escape and be mated to another dog during the remainder of her season. We once knew of a bitch who, having been mated normally on the twelfth day of her season, escaped on the twenty-first day, and produced a litter of mongrel puppies, which shows that one can never generalise about the best date in the season to mate!

No special treatment of the bitch is necessary during the first four or five weeks following the mating, and she should be encouraged to lead a normal life. She may start to show signs of being in whelp as early as the fifth week, a tightness behind the ribs being noticeable, and swelling and pink colouration of the teats (not the teeth, as a lady of our acquaintance once earnestly assured us!). Slight moistness of the vulva is also often observed in a pregnant bitch. Pregnancy diagnosis in maiden bitches, and in bitches carrying small litters, is often difficult, and some keep their owners guessing throughout the pregancy. However anxious to know the truth one may be, it is unwise to allow a vet to palpate and prod a bitch in order to diagnose possible pregnancy. He can so easily be wrong, and it does the bitch no good. St Bernard puppies are small in proportion to the size of their dam, and quite large litters have been known to arrive without any prior signs of their presence.

The expectant mother, whether showing in whelp or not, should have her rations gradually increased, and a good mineral additive should be included in the diet. Cod-liver oil is important as a source of vitamins A and D, and can be given in capsule form if the bitch dislikes the taste. Carrots are an excellent source of vitamin C, and will protect the bitch and litter against skin troubles. Vitamin E, the fertility vitamin, is plentiful in wheat-germ oil, eggs, milk and fish.

An in-whelp bitch always drinks copiously, and a supply of fresh, clean drinking water should always be available.

From the sixth week of pregnancy it is advisable to divide the bitch's food into two helpings, giving a small meal in the morning, and the main meal in the evening. The emphasis now should be on high-protein rations such a meat and milk, without allowing the bitch to get too fat by feeding excess carbohydrate. At this stage she should be segregated from other dogs, in case rough play or over-strenuous exercise damages the developing litter.

A few days prior to the expected date of whelping her vulva and underbody should be well washed with a mild disinfectant, and excess hair on hind legs and the underside of the tail should be trimmed away. At this stage the bitch should be introduced to her whelping quarters.

WHELPING QUARTERS

The room where the bitch is to have her puppies should be either within the house, or easily accessible from it. Nothing is more annoying, especially in winter, than trudging backwards and forwards to an outbuilding during the night to supervise a bitch and her puppies. Most bitches appreciate the reassurance of human company at this time, and, after the puppies are born, it is a great advantage to have them within earshot, so that the cries of any in distress can be easily heard.

A whelping box for a St Bernard should be at least 4 ft by 3 ft, and the construction of one should not be beyond the capabilities of the average handyman. It is a good plan to have one of the longer sides hinged, so that when the puppies are older it can be let down to form a ramp. The box should be fitted with a metal guard-rail, similar to a pig farrowing rail, to prevent any puppy pushed against the side from being overlain.

WHELPING-BOX (at least 4' by 3')

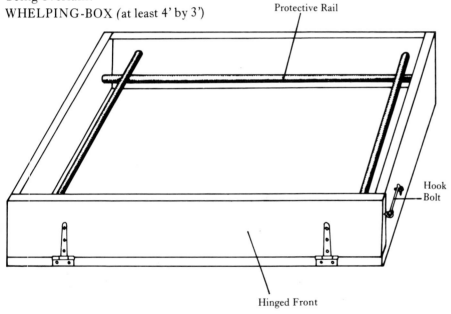

Protective Rail

Whelping Box

Hook
Bolt

Hinged Front

The best form of bedding is clean newspapers, and every paper coming into the house should be saved for this purpose, as an enormous quantity will be needed. It is a simple matter to roll the soiled paper up and renew with clean when necessary. Polyester fur rugs, often advertised for whelping purposes, are impractical for St Bernards, as the large sizes necessary make washing and drying a problem.

The room where the birth is to take place should be heated to at least

$21°C(70°F)$. An infra-red lamp, suspended out of the bitch's reach above the whelping box, makes an ideal heater, but in winter other background heating in the room will probably be needed. Newly born puppies must be kept snug and warm, but the bitch should not be too hot or she may become distressed, and try to lie away from her puppies.

First-aid items which may be needed during the whelping include a sharp pair of blunt-nosed scissors, a reel of strong cotton, plenty of old clean towels, and some Vaseline. A supply of glucose and a small plastic syringe will be useful should it be necessary to give fluid to the puppies during a long whelping. It is always advisable to prepare a large roomy box, or carton, lined with blankets, and containing a stone hot-water bottle wrapped in a woollen cover. If this is kept ready in a warm spot, you will have somewhere to put the puppies if you need to remove any from the bitch while she is in labour.

WHELPING

The gestation period of 63 days is counted from the day following the mating, but it is not unusual for a bitch to give birth two or three days before or after the anticipated date. Should she be more than five days over her time however, it may be an indication that all is not well. The table opposite shows expected whelping dates for given mating dates.

Prior to the birth the mother will become very restless, ripping and scratching at her bed of newspaper, and panting increasingly heavily. When the birth is imminent there will be a pale green discharge from the vulva, which will be swollen, indicating that the cervix (neck) of the womb has begun to dilate. Should the discharge be of an obnoxious dark brown or black colour, rather than green, the presence of dead puppies is indicated, and the vet should be sent for at once. A bitch will normally refuse all food during the twenty-four hours prior to whelping, and her body temperature will fall to below $37.8°C(100°F)$, which is nature's way of preparing the puppies to face the cooler environment outside their mother's body.

It is most important for the owner, or person attending the bitch, to keep calm and unflurried during the whelping proceedings. Agitation on the owner's part so easily communicates itself to the bitch, who has enough to cope with anyway without the presence of a distraught owner. We were once asked to go to assist at the whelping of a Saint bitch belonging to some friends. When we arrived we found the entire family, including four children, all gathered around the whelping place, waiting for the first puppy to appear! The quieter you can keep the bitch, and the less you interfere and break the natural bond between mother and puppies, the better for all concerned.

If all is proceeding normally the bitch will start to strain at

Served Jan. Whelps March	Served Feb. Whelps April	Served March Whelps May	Served April Whelps June	Served May Whelps July	Served June Whelps Aug.	Served July Whelps Sept.	Served Aug. Whelps Oct.	Served Sept. Whelps Nov.	Served Oct. Whelps Dec.	Served Nov. Whelps Jan.	Served Dec. Whelps Feb.
1 5	1 5	1 3	1 3	1 3	1 3	1 2	1 3	1 3	1 3	1 3	1 2
2 6	2 6	2 4	2 4	2 4	2 4	2 3	2 4	2 4	2 4	2 4	2 3
3 7	3 7	3 5	3 5	3 5	3 5	3 4	3 5	3 5	3 5	3 5	3 4
4 8	4 8	4 6	4 6	4 6	4 6	4 5	4 6	4 6	4 6	4 6	4 5
5 9	5 9	5 7	5 7	5 7	5 7	5 6	5 7	5 7	5 7	5 7	5 6
6 10	6 10	6 8	6 8	6 8	6 8	6 7	6 8	6 8	6 8	6 8	6 7
7 11	7 11	7 9	7 9	7 9	7 9	7 8	7 9	7 9	7 9	7 9	7 8
8 12	8 12	8 10	8 10	8 10	8 10	8 9	8 10	8 10	8 10	8 10	8 9
9 13	9 13	9 11	9 11	9 11	9 11	9 10	9 11	9 11	9 11	9 11	9 10
10 14	10 14	10 12	10 12	10 12	10 12	10 11	10 12	10 12	10 12	10 12	10 11
11 15	12 15	11 13	11 13	11 13	11 13	11 12	11 13	11 13	11 13	11 13	11 12
12 16	13 16	12 14	12 14	12 14	12 14	12 13	12 14	12 14	12 14	12 14	12 13
13 17	14 17	13 15	13 15	13 15	13 15	13 14	13 15	13 15	13 15	13 15	13 14
14 18	15 18	14 16	14 16	14 16	14 16	14 15	14 16	14 16	14 16	14 16	14 15
15 19	16 19	15 17	15 17	15 17	15 17	15 16	15 17	15 17	15 17	15 17	15 16
16 20	17 20	16 18	16 18	16 18	16 18	16 17	16 18	16 18	16 18	16 18	16 17
17 21	18 21	17 19	17 19	17 19	17 19	17 18	17 19	17 19	17 19	17 19	17 18
18 22	19 22	18 20	18 20	18 20	18 20	18 19	18 20	18 20	18 20	18 20	18 19
19 23	20 23	19 21	19 21	19 21	19 21	19 20	19 21	19 21	19 21	19 21	19 20
20 24	21 24	20 22	20 22	20 22	20 22	20 21	20 22	20 22	20 22	20 22	20 21
21 25	22 25	21 23	21 23	21 23	21 23	21 22	21 23	21 23	21 23	21 23	21 22
22 26	23 26	22 24	22 24	22 24	22 24	22 23	22 24	22 24	22 24	22 24	22 23
23 27	24 27	23 25	23 25	23 25	23 25	23 24	23 25	23 25	23 25	23 25	23 24
24 28	25 28	24 26	24 26	24 26	24 26	24 25	24 26	24 26	24 26	24 26	24 25
25 29	26 29	25 27	25 27	25 27	25 27	25 26	25 27	25 27	25 27	25 27	25 26
26 30	27 30	26 28	26 28	26 28	26 28	26 27	26 28	26 28	26 28	26 28	26 27
27 31	28 1	27 29	27 29	27 29	27 29	27 28	27 29	27 29	27 29	27 29	27 28
28 1	29 2	28 30	28 30	28 30	28 30	28 29	28 30	28 30	28 30	28 30	28 1
29 2		29 31	29 1	29 31	29 31	29 30	29 31	29 1	29 31	29 31	29 2
30 3		30 1	30 2	30 1	30 1	30 1	30 1	30 2	30 1	30 1	30 3
31 4		31 2		31 2		31 2	31 2		31 2		31 4

Whelping dates for given mating dates.

increasingly frequent regular intervals, and within an hour the first puppy should appear, preceded by a sudden flow of greenish fluid which is released when the water sac surrounding the puppy breaks, just prior to its birth. The bitch should lick the foetal membrane away from the puppy's face, and bite through the umbilical cord, but, should she fail to do so, the assistant must quickly free the puppy's breathing passages, and, after ligaturing the cord with thread, sever it with sterilised scissors. A good rub with a warm towel will help to dry the puppy, and stimulate its heart and lungs, and, if then put to a teat, it should make attempts to suck. It is most important, when a maiden bitch gives birth to her first puppy, to try to let her do as much for it herself as possible, after quietly freeing the membrane from its face yourself, so that it can breathe. She has to learn her maternal duties, and the sooner she is allowed to do so the better.

Each puppy should be followed by its afterbirth, which is the placenta through which its blood and that of its mother came in contact. The bitch should be allowed to eat some, if not all, of the afterbirths, as they form a valuable source of iron and protein, and assist in milk production.

If all is going normally the bitch should soon start to strain again, and further puppies will be produced. If the litter is large, and the whelping protracted, it is sometimes advisable to remove some of the first-born puppies to the warm box which you have prepared, as they tend to get wet and chilled while the later members of the litter are being born. Try to do this as unobtrusively as possible, and put them out of the bitch's earshot. If they have already had a suck from their mother, they will cuddle up to their warm bottle, and go contendedly to sleep, leaving the mother free to concentrate on those born later. When the puppies start to suck, reflex contractions are set up in the uterus, which assist in expelling those yet unborn. The interval between the birth of each puppy often lengthens towards the end of the whelping, and this is the time when the dam will probably welcome a warm drink of milk, or glucose and water, to sustain her strength. The bed will get very soggy and wet, and should be renewed with clean papers whenever a suitable opportunity occurs. The mother may wish to go outside to relieve herself several times during the whelping, and this is the time to watch her closely, as the activity may cause her to drop a puppy outside.

St Bernards are slower whelpers than many other breeds, possibly because the puppies, weighing on average 1½–2 lb, are relatively small in proportion to the size of the dam, and do not so greatly stimulate uterine contractions. If the bitch strains strongly for over an hour without a puppy being produced, it is an indication that help is necessary. There may be a blockage due to two puppies trying to pass through the cervix simultaneously, or possibly a puppy is being presented feet first, which is known as a breach birth, and can cause trouble. If the vet is sent for, he will probably give the bitch an injection of 2 ml of the hormone pituitrin, which will make the uterine contractions intensify, and usually cause a puppy to be expelled within twenty minutes. If pituitrin is unsuccessful, internal examination and possibly manipulation may be necessary, but this should never be attempted by the inexperienced novice.

Caesarian operations
If the bitch cannot produce her puppies normally, and does not respond to injections, the vet may advise a Caesarean operation, which should be carried out as soon as possible if any puppies within are to be saved. With modern antibiotics there is little risk in this operation, provided it is not delayed too long. The vet will anaesthetise the bitch

and withdraw the puppies through an incision in the abdominal wall and uterus. It is always advisable for the owner to be on hand if this operation has to take place, as much stimulation may be necessary to get the puppies breathing after this form of birth, and the vet may be too preoccupied with the dam to have time to attend to the babies himself. Most bitches suckle their litter normally after a Caesarian operation, but if the milk is slow to appear in the teats, it may be necessary to feed the puppies by hand for the first few hours until the dam is well enough to take over. As a temporary measure, a weak solution of glucose and water, passed slowly into their mouths with a small syringe, is preferable to a milk feed at this stage.

After whelping

Once the whelping is over, the bitch will relax with her puppies, and she should be kept as quiet as possible and allowed to rest.

One is often asked how many puppies can be expected from a St Bernard bitch! The average would appear to be between eight and ten, although a St Bernard in America is reported to have produced a world record of 23. A famous litter in this country was born in February 1895 to the bitch Lady Millard, who was owned by Mr Thorpe of Northwold. It consisted of 21 puppies, but there is no record of how many were reared! The bitch, and not the stud dog, governs the number of puppies in any litter, as it depends on the number of eggs released from the ovaries.

10 Care of the Bitch and her Puppies

Once the problems of birth have been overcome, one is faced with an even more demanding and difficult task, that of rearing the litter! It is one matter to produce the puppies, but quite another to rear them so well that all grow into sound, healthy St Bernards which will be a credit to breeder and breed.

After the whelping, the bitch should be taken outside to relieve herself, and while she is away from the puppies, the chance can be taken to renew her bed. She should then be given a warm, milky, drink and allowed to return to her litter. She will soon relax happily with them, and can now be allowed to rest undisturbed.

The following day the bitch should have her tail and back quarters well washed with warm, soapy, water; she must be thoroughly rinsed and dried before being returned to her nest. This cleaning will probably have to be repeated several times during the week following the birth.

For the first day after the whelping, the bitch should be kept on milk diet, to which eggs and glucose can be added. If she will eat it, she can then go onto a light diet of cooked tripe, fish, chicken, rabbit etc. together with plenty of milk, and, of course, fresh water. She will drink copiously throughout her lactation. At about the fourth day, she can return to a more normal diet, but the quantities must be gradually increased until she is having at least twice her normal rations, and plenty of milk and eggs. For a St Bernard bitch nursing a large litter five feeds daily, with liberal mineral and vitamin additives, are not excessive. If the bitch is at first reluctant to leave her puppies, as many are, the food must be placed before her in the nest.

If a bitch refuses food in the days following the whelping, or runs temperature and seems in any way 'off colour', it may be an indication that all is not well. Sometimes a retained afterbirth, or a dead puppy inside, can cause trouble, and if there is any anxiety, the vet should be called. He will probably give an antibiotic and an injection of pituitrin which will stimulate uterine contractions and cause anything remaining in the womb to be expelled.

There are few more pleasing sights than a St Bernard bitch nursing contented litter of puppies when all is going well. Constant crying is a danger signal, and means that the puppies are either cold – they need a temperature of at least 21°C (70°F) – or that they are hungry. If a puppy is having sufficient milk, its belly should feel rounded and plump, and it should not be constantly shifting from teat to teat in search of more food. In some bitches, especially maidens, the milk may be slow to come down into the teats, and the flow may have to be stimulated with pituitrin and other drugs. If there is a shortage of milk, it will be necessary to feed the puppies partly or entirely by hand, as described later in this chapter. Never give up hope, however; we once had a bitch of another breed, who, after her puppies had been on the bottle for over a week, suddenly demanded them, produced milk, and decided to feed them!

Controversy has always raged about whether a St Bernard puppy should have its dew-claws removed. Some breeders consider that, if they are left on, the dew-claws increase the massive appearance of the hind feet, and that their removal weakens the hind action of the adult dog. According to the English Standard they should be removed; if not, they can cause much trouble later; they tear easily, and in older dogs can become ingrown and infected. In our opinion, the dew-claws should be removed from both front and back limbs when the puppies are five days old. Many breeders undertake this task themselves, but novices are wise to leave it to a vet, as a bungled job can make removal of the claws under anaesthetic necessary at a later date. While the operation is being performed, the bitch should be taken for a walk out of ear-shot, so that she is not distressed by the cries of her offspring. The vet should make sure that there is no bleeding, and after the operation, the puppies should be placed in a clean bed, to avert infection of the wounds. They will scream loudly with *momentary* pain while the deed is being done, but, the operation is not truly painful, and when the mother returns, they will soon suckle happily, having forgotten all about it.

The puppies' eyes should open at about ten days, and their ears about a week later. It is sadly not infrequent for St Bernard puppies to be overlain and squashed by their dam, and this often happens when they are about ten days old and start climbing over and under the mother's body. The mother sleeps so heavily that she is often deaf to the cries of her distressed offspring. A pig-rail round the whelping bed does help to overcome this problem, but, short of staying with the puppies throughout the 24 hours of day and night, it is a tragedy that cannot be avoided.

If the litter is large and there is competition for the best teats, some bitches can get very scratched and sore on the belly, due to the action of the puppies' sharp, needle-like claws. If this occurs the nails can be gently trimmed at the tips (not in the quicks) with a pair of sharp scissors. With small litters, there is sometimes a problem when the milk is not sucked from certain teats, which may make the glands hard and inflamed. In this case, the teats concerned may have to be gently bathed with warm water and the milk withdrawn by hand.

WEANING
The age of weaning will depend on the number in the litter and on the condition of the mother. If she is at all pulled down physically by her task, which she should not be if her diet is adequate, it is as well to begin to wean when the litter is between two and three weeks old.

The weaning process cannot be too gradual. The first feed should consist of about half an ounce (28 g) of finely minced raw meat, rolled into a ball and given by hand to each puppy. It is amazing how quickly a St Bernard puppy learns to accept this and attempts to snatch it from one's fingers! After giving this once daily for two or three days, a small milk feed can be introduced, and the puppies gently taught to lap. They will get in a terrible mess at first, but soon learn the knack, and will be eager to lick any surplus from the faces of their litter-mates.

There are many substitutes for bitches' milk, and all breeders have their own ideas about which is best used at weaning. Any milk used must be as close in composition to that of the bitch as possible, which means that it must be extremely high in protein, solids, and fat. As will be seen from the following table, cows' milk is quite unsuitable in composition to give to young puppies.

Kind of Milk	Water %	Total solids %	Protein	Fat	Carbohydrates	Other solids
Bitch	75.4	24.6	11.2	9.6	3.1	0.7
Cow	87.2	12.8	3.5	3.7	4.9	0.7
Goat	85.7	14.3	4.3	4.8	4.4	0.8

The best natural substitute for bitches' milk is goats' milk, which can be purchased from many health food stores; failing this, one of the proprietary puppy milks on the market can be given, or baby milk mixed at slightly increased strength. We have always used goats' milk or, if this has been unavailable, Gold Top Calf Milk, mixed at 50% above the recommended strength. Owing to the low carbohydrate content of bitches' milk, we do not believe in adding glucose to the weaning milk, as it increases the sugar content too much. If one must sweeten the milk, honey is a better additive, as it is rich in vitamins.

As the gradual weaning process continues the bitch should be kept away from her puppies for longer and more frequent intervals, and their new meals should be made more frequent. By the age of four or five weeks, they should be having four daily feeds, two of minced raw meat, and two of milk. At this stage, raw egg yolk, and a few drops of cod-liver oil can be added to the meat feeds, and the milk feeds can include baby cereals such as Farex and Farlene. These latter are rich in calcium and other minerals, and while they are being fed we do not consider it necessary to give other mineral additives. A good puppy biscuit can gradually be introduced, mixed into the meat.

At the last stage of weaning, it is advisable to allow the bitch to sleep with her puppies, and be separated from them for the remainder of the 24 hours, as they then have the comfort of the natural milk bar during the long night interval.

It is a good plan to have the puppies completely weaned by six or seven weeks of age, so that they have ample time to adjust themselves to the complete absence of their mother before they leave for their new homes at 8 weeks.

WORMING

Most puppies harbour a few round worms, although St Bernards do not seem to become so badly infected as some of the smaller breeds. The sooner these worms are eliminated the better, and the first treatment can take place at between three and four weeks. We have always used Coopane tablets, obtainable from a vet, and have never found the puppies to suffer ill-effect; in fact, after the first dosing, they always appear to make increasingly rapid progress, even if no worms are evident. The puppies should be wormed a second time at 6 weeks, and again two weeks later, if worms have been observed.

ROUGHS AND SMOOTHS

If one of the parents is smooth-coated, it is probable that the litter will contain puppies of each coat type, but which are which will not be obvious until about 6 weeks. The difference is usually first apparent on the underside of the tail and on the backs of the thighs. In Rough puppies these soon begin to fluff-up and appear bushy, but remain flat in the Smooths.

HAND REARING PUPPIES

For various reasons, it may be necessary to rear some or all of a litter of puppies by hand, and it is a time-consuming and tiring task, only to be attempted if no alternative is available. If the dam dies, or is unable to feed the puppies, it is sometimes possible to locate a bitch of another large breed, who may be able to foster them. Years ago, the canine magazines frequently carried advertisements from firms who made a business of supplying foster mothers, usually mongrel bitches whose own puppies had been destroyed. Happily this cruel trade has now ceased. We once reared three terrier puppies on a St Bernard, who had only four of her own, but it was an anxious time, and we could not leave them with her without supervision.

Puppies obtain anti-bodies against infection from the dam's early milk, which is known as colostrum, and puppies bottle-reared from birth will lack this protection, and be initially more prone to succumb to infection.

If it is decided to bottle-rear, the first essential is a warm box, ideally under an infra-red lamp, which avoids the chore of constantly re-filling hot water bottles. The lamp should be hung at a height which ensures a comfortably warm temperature. If the puppies huddle together below it, it shows they are too cold, and the lamp should be lowered.

At first, the puppies will need feeding every two hours of the day and night, and meal times must be regular. We use a 5 ml plastic injection syringe (without, of course, the needle!) and give 2 ml of milk per feed. The syringe enables the milk to be slowly dripped into the mouth, and after a few feeds the puppies will soon begin to enjoy their meals. They will then try to suck from the syringe, and make reflex pummelling movements with their front legs. This is the time to begin to use a baby's teat on the end of the syringe, pushing the milk gently into the teat and controlling the flow with the plunger.

A proprietary brand of puppy milk, such as Lactol, can be used for bottle rearing, and a supply of this should be mixed fresh for every feed, and given at blood heat. Goats' milk is a better answer to the problem, as it is less inclined to clog the teat, and puppies reared on it always seem less prone to enteritis than those given reconstituted powdered milk. For the first few feeds it is wise to dilute the milk slightly.

After each feed the puppies must each have their bladders and bowels activated, a task which would normally be performed by the licking action of the mother's tongue. If the tummy and anus are gently massaged with a soft tissue or pad of cotton wool (and a great deal of patience) it should be possible to achieve the evacuation. If the puppies become constipated, a few drops of olive oil in the milk will help to loosen the bowels, and, as a last resort, the carefully Vaselined tip of a clinical thermometer, gently rotated in the rectum, will often stimulate the necessary movement.

Faces and back-ends should be gently sponged daily to keep the puppies sweet smelling. The syringe and teat used for feeding must be kept scrupulously clean.

The quantity of milk given at each feed can be gradually increased as the puppies grow. After a meal their tummies should feel comfortably full, but not bloated, and one must be careful not to over-feed. If they are having sufficient, the puppies should sleep contentedly until their next meal is due. At the end of the second week it should be possible to change to three-hourly feeding, and to miss a feed during the night so that you get some rest. They can now have a little scraped raw beef daily, and should soon be able to lap. Once this stage is reached, exhausted but triumphant, you will feel the worthwhile battle has been won!

CARE OF THE BITCH AFTER REARING A LITTER

When the bitch is weaned from her puppies she should not be a pulled-down wreck, but, however well you have fed her, she will have lost condition, and will need extra feeding and care for some time to rebuild her strength. If she is weaned before the puppies are too large, her undercarriage should not be spoiled, and its retraction can be assisted by gently rubbing the glands with surgical spirit.

Most bitches have a full moult following a litter, and their coats do not come back into show condition for about six months.

A bitch will normally come into season again four months after her puppies were born, but she should never be mated on this season, as she is not a puppy machine, and one litter per year is ample for a St Bernard.

New Homes for Puppies

Even more difficult than breeding and rearing a litter of St Bernards is finding suitable homes for the puppies. You were responsible for bringing them into the world, and it is your duty to see them settled with families able to give them the time, training, and attention needed by such large dogs. Mistakes at this time can lead later to unhappy, unwanted dogs, regarded as nuisances, and eventually perhaps destroyed because no one can cope with them. If you dodge your responsibilities in this matter now, you are as bad as the 'puppy factories' who breed solely on a commercial basis, without regard for the betterment of the breed, or the welfare of the unfortunate animals they bring into existence.

Although it may seem impertinent at the time, you must question prospective St Bernard buyers closely about their personal circumstances, and their reasons for wanting a St Bernard. So often the dog is really only desired as a status symbol, who will be rejected when the disadvantages of his presence in the household become apparent. It is always revealing to enquire if the family have previously owned a dog, and, if so, what happened to it, and how long it lived. One should beware of buyers with very small children, who may have little time and affection left for a St Bernard. Homes where all the family go out to work are also to be avoided, as the dog will be alone for most of the time.

Before definitely promising a puppy, you should always meet the prospective new owners personally, and, if in doubt, try to visit their homes and judge for yourself if a St Bernard is likely to fit in to the scheme of things.

If the new owners seem suitable, try to tell them all you can about the advantages and disadvantages of the breed. Those who really wish to do their best for the dog they are buying, will be only too keen to learn. When selling a puppy it is always wise to ask the new owner to return it to you, should it be necessary to part with it for any unforeseen reason. You can then yourself ensure that it is placed in a suitable alternative home.

When you sell a puppy always supply a diet sheet, and explain this carefully to the new owner. It is a good plan to allow the puppy to leave with a day's supply of his usual food, as he will not then have to cope with an immediate change of both diet and environment. Always ask buyers to let you know how the puppy has settled down, and offer to give information in the future should any queries arise. The puppy should also take with him his pedigree, and Kennel Club documents, if any.

Kennel Club Registration

Before puppies can be registered at the Kennel Club, it is necessary to record the birth of the litter. Application for Litter Recording is made on K. C. Form 1, and, among other particulars, requires the signature of the stud dog's owner.

Under a new system introduced in October 1978, it is possible for a breeder to register any or all of a litter of puppies, at the same time as application is made for Recording. A breeder who is the owner of a registered affix (kennel name) may wish to do this, so that the puppies will carry his affix. If not, he will receive from the Kennel Club a separate application form for each puppy in the litter, which can be used for registration at a later date.

When selling puppies which are likely to be exhibited, it is obviously desirable to register them in one's own affix. Pet puppies can either be sold unregistered, or the buyers be given the forms to make application themselves should they choose to do so. If it is agreed at the time of purchase that the puppy is being bought solely as a pet, a breeder, having registered it, can return the Registration Card to the Kennel Club to be endorsed in any or all of the following ways: (1) not eligible for Entry at Shows; (2) progeny not eligible for registration; (3) not eligible for the issue of an Export Pedigree; (4) name unchangeable.

Before a registered dog can be exhibited or bred from, he must be transferred at the Kennel Club into the name of his new owner. Application for this should be made on K. C. Form 6.

11 On Choosing a St Bernard Puppy

'Of course, we only want a pet!'

So many times this is said by would-be St Bernard purchasers, searching for their first puppy, and at the time it is usually true. However, such is their pride in the achievement of acquiring and rearing their first Saint, and so complimentary are the remarks of their friends, that soon a tremendous sense of kudos has arisen. They are persuaded, often against their better judgement, to take the puppy to a small local show, where perhaps the standard of competition is not high, and they come away with a card. Now they are 'hooked', and the dog showing world has another recruit, and the Kennel Club a further potential source of revenue. Even the strong-minded purchaser, who will not under any circumstances be tempted to exhibit the puppy bought as a friend and companion, will wish this new member of the family to be a healthy and typical specimen of its breed, so some guidance on what to look for when choosing a St Bernard puppy is essential.

A fine pre-war litter by Ch. Beldene Bruno, out of Miss Pratt's Ch. Berndean Ailsa. Ch. Berndean Invader is third from the left.

Never buy any puppy, especially a St Bernard, in a hurry. The purchase of a puppy is like a contract which should last throughout its life, and will entail obligations on your part in terms of time, money, and adaptation of life-style. The larger the dog, the greater will these commitments be, and in the case of a St Bernard they should not be entered into without the most careful thought and understanding by all members of the family.

Once you have decided that you are a suitable individual or family to be owned by a St Bernard, the search for the right puppy can begin. One can obtain a list of reputable breeders from the Kennel Club, or scan the advertisement columns of the weekly magazines *Dog World* and *Our Dogs*. *The Dog Directory* is available from book sellers, or directly from Binfield Park, Bracknell, Berkshire, and contains lists of kennels dealing in most breeds. It is an excellent plan to try to attend one of the larger dog shows, where there may be classes for St Bernards, as this will give the opportunity to meet and talk with breeders, and study their dogs.

Unfortunately, there are those with St Bernards, as with all other breeds, who having bought a bitch puppy at what seems to them a high price, imagine that, by breeding from this bitch, and selling, they hope, a large litter at a similar price, they will make their fortune! In many cases they mate the bitch to the nearest available dog, often not a show specimen, and find the resultant litter difficult to dispose of. As the puppies get larger, the appetites increase, and very often there are neighbour problems, as a result of the playful yapping with which a vigorous litter often likes to greet the dawn. In desperation, such litters, or the less attractive members of them, are often sold cheaply to dealers, who then offer them to the public at inflated prices. If purchasing a puppy from someone who is not the breeder it pays to be very cautious. Pet shops and firms advertising puppies of all and every breed for sale, have seldom bred the animals they handle, and for a young puppy to pass to its new owner via the agency of a middle-man in itself constitutes a danger to the puppy's health and development. To rear at St Bernard puppy well is a knowledgeable and expensive task, and if the foundations of sound rearing have not been laid early in the puppy's life the leeway is difficult, if not impossible, to make up.

Before the search for a suitable puppy begins, the prospective owner must decide whether a Rough or Smooth St Bernard is desired, and whether a dog or bitch.

Smooths, or short-haired St Bernards, are less often seen in Britain than on the Continent and in America, but they have their adherents, and their use is essential in serious breeding programmes. Rough puppies look more attractive and cuddlesome, but one must remember that their coats require more attention. There is more hair shed when a

Three Smooth
puppies from the
Peldartor Kennels.

Rough St Bernard casts its coat, and a Rough will always bring more mud and dirt into the house than its Smooth counterpart. It is easier to win in the show ring with Roughs, as the coat can camouflage structural defects and imperfections. Smooths often tend to be lighter-boned than Roughs, and in some cases can be very 'shelly' looking, but, in the writers' opinion, a really good Smooth, showing the correct head type and conformation, coupled with the desired height and bone, is a dog without equal.

The question of the puppy's sex needs very careful consideration. If there is no intention of breeding, many families prefer a male animal, to avoid the inconvenience of seasons. Pet females can always be spayed, but this is a fairly expensive operation, not without risk, and may result in a tendency to obesity unless one diets very carefully. It is said females make more gentle and docile pets, but the most gentle-natured St Bernard we have personally owned has been a male, and one of the most tomboyish a bitch, so one cannot generalise! Occasionally some male dogs tend to become rather too amorous and over-sexed, which can prove embarassing. One point worthy of mention is the fact that a fully grown St Bernard male will be much heavier and more powerful than a bitch, and if the new owner, or the person who will have to spend most time with the animal, is a woman, the decision should possibly be in favour of a bitch. Even in these enlightened days of Women's Lib, few of the fair sex have the strength to act as sheet anchor to a fourteen-stone St Bernard, intent on setting off in an undesired direction. One knows that, in theory, all dogs should be so well trained that these mishaps never occur, but with some owners, however earnest the intention, the gift of instilling complete obedience is sadly lacking.

Having decided on the sex and coat-type of the puppy one hopes to acquire, it is probably a good idea to visit several kennels and look at litters and adults. Most breeders are only too willing to show off their stock, even if not for sale, and the majority are happy to give advice to those who genuinely wish to learn. It is always wise to telephone first for an appointment, as breeders are busy people, and you may not receive a very warm reception if you arrive in the midst of feeding time. Most genuine breeders are very anxious to ensure that those purchasing stock from them will make suitable St Bernard owners, and you must not be surprised if you are questioned about your reasons for wanting a Saint, and the facilities you can provide for its care.

All puppies are attractive, St Bernard puppies exceptionally so, and a new purchaser must not allow himself to be so carried away by enthusiasm for the appealing youngsters that he loses his critical faculties. Notice whether puppies and runs are reasonably clean. All puppies soil their pens, but several days accumulation of excrement is a bad sign, as is any indication of diarrhoea. Healthy puppies should have bright eyes, without discharge; their noses should be moist and cool, but not runny; they should not be pot-bellied or have sores on their abdomens. St Bernard puppies should look massive, even at the age of six or eight weeks, when their weight should be about 15 lb, and their legs should be thick and well-boned. They should be alert and friendly, but do not automatically dismiss one who appears more interested in sleep than making a good impression. He could be just resting after a spell of boisterous play or an extra good meal.

One should always be honest with a breeder about whether a puppy is being bought as a prospective show prospect or solely as a pet. In our opinion it is impossible to state at 8 weeks whether a youngster is a 'show puppy', or not; one can only select from a litter the one which appears at that early age to be most promising from a show point of view. If you tell a breeder that you may wish to exhibit your new purchase when he is old enough, you should receive assistance in selecting one of the more promising members of the litter, but you must understand that no guarantee can be given, as so much will depend on how the puppy grows and how well you are able to rear it. If you choose one of the better show-prospects among a litter of puppies, you must expect to pay a slightly increased price for it. Nothing is more annoying, however, to a breeder than to sell a puppy as a pet, at pet price, and later see the same puppy damaging the reputation of his kennels in the show-ring. Fortunately, it is now possible for a breeder

to place Kennel Club endorsements on a puppy's registration documents, so that it cannot be shown, or its puppies registered; if you buy
a pet puppy you must expect to find that this has been done.

In picking a puppy as a show prospect, the first consideration should
be the head. This should be large in proportion to the size of the dog,
and have a well-defined 'stop', that is, there should be almost a right
angle where the skull rises from the top of the muzzle. The muzzle
should look short, and be broad and flat across its bridge. It should
look square when viewed from the front, in fact like a small square
block on the front of the face. When gripped between the ears the skull
should feel wide, in fact wider than the width of the muzzle. The bite
should be carefully checked. A slightly overshot mouth at this age is
not a bad point, as when the lower jaw develops, and the larger second
teeth come through, the bite should be level. An undershot jaw,
however, will never improve, and will tend to worsen as the puppy
grows older. It will be a handicap in the show ring, but if the puppy is
being bought as a pet, it is an imperfection that could be overlooked.
At seven weeks the eyes should be as dark as possible, a sort of slate
colour. If they appear blue, they will be much too light in later life.
The ears should not be too big, and the nose and lips should be black.

The late A. K.
Gaunt with one of
his Cornagarth St
Bernard puppies.

Right: Mrs
Kathleen Gaunt.

A promising St Bernard puppy, showing broad, round skull, strong, square muzzle, and pronounced stop.

It is important to watch the puppies move around, and check that they put their feet down facing straight ahead. Try to pick a well-angulated puppy, and avoid one that appears cow-hocked, although allowance must be made for a general looseness of limb at this age.

It is sometimes difficult to tell by seven weeks which puppies are Smooths and which Roughs. The darker the puppy's coat colour, the richer red it will eventually become. If the puppy appeals in other respects, one should not be too fussy about its markings, provided the chest, forelegs and end of tail are white. The head should be evenly marked with a white blaze up the centre, but this will tend to close in as the puppy grows, and if narrow it may disappear altogether. In the writers' opinion, markings are of secondary importance to type and conformation, and one should hesitate to discard an otherwise good puppy should, for example, its white collar be incomplete.

One is often asked what price can reasonably be expected for a St Bernard puppy. At the end of 1986, £250 to £400 were fair average figures, depending on age, show potential, pedigree and whether inoculated. With costs escalating as they are doing at the moment, prices must inevitably increase. St Bernards are expensive to keep, and if one finds the initial outlay daunting, the rearing and maintenance costs may also be beyond one's means; and it might be more sensible to choose a smaller breed.

12 The Rearing and Care of St Bernards

Most breeders will not allow puppies to go to their new homes until they are 8 weeks old, by which time they should be well used to living apart from their mothers. Before the great day for collecting the new member of the family arrives, certain important preparations must be made. The garden must be securely fenced, and any ornamental ponds made inaccessible. Heavy garden ornaments which might fall, or be pulled down, causing injury to the puppy, should be removed. In the house, any dangling electric flexes should be put out of reach. It will be sensible to restrict the puppy at first, until he is house trained, to one room, possibly the kitchen, and a special corner should be prepared here for his sleeping quarters. If it is planned to confine the puppy to any form of pen, this should be sufficiently high (or roofed) to eliminate any risk of him climbing out, and injuring himself.

Stocks of food for the new inmate must be bought in, and it is a good plan to telephone the breeder for advice as to what to purchase. The lady of the house should also get on very friendly terms with the butcher! The breeder should be told what time you will be fetching the puppy, and asked not to feed him for several hours before he is due to travel (to prevent travel sickness).

When the new puppy is collected, the purchaser should be supplied with his pedigree, and the Kennel Club documents, if available. As mentioned in the previous chapter, if the puppy is being bought as a pet, the Kennel Club Registration Card may be endorsed to the effect that he is not to be shown or bred from.

Travelling by car is a new and frightening experience for a young puppy, and he may be car-sick during the journey. In any case, it is wise to travel with a good supply of old newspapers in case of emergency.

The move to a new home is an enormous disruption in a puppy's young life, as not only will he miss the companionship of his litter mates, but he will have many new experiences to face and new people to meet. He will probably be very quiet for the first few hours, while he is summing up his new owners, and growing accustomed to his surroundings. Try not to fuss over him at this stage, but let him settle down quietly on his own. When his confidence has been gained, he will soon come seeking affection and play.

Training

A poorly trained dog of any breed reflects discredit on his owner, and an uncontrollable St Bernard is a menace to all with whom he comes in contact. Neurotic dogs are usually the fault of excitable and erratic owners; in fact, one can usually judge the temperament of the owner by that of the dog. A young St Bernard puppy must be treated with kind firmness from the word go, and must not be permitted to do things as a puppy which will be unacceptable when he is fully grown.

An eight-week-old puppy will not be house trained, so accidents must be expected. These can be minimised by taking him to a regular spot in the garden, conveniently near the back door, at frequent intervals, (*every time* after meals and immediately he wakes from sleep). It requires patience, but if the owner can find the time to remain with him outside to praise and make a great fuss of him as soon as he has 'obliged', and then take him back into the house, he should soon learn to be clean. It is unlikely that an eight-week-old puppy will manage to contain himself throughout the night, so a thick pad of newspaper near

Dogs of the Mount St Bernard Abbey in Charnwood Forest.

the door will be necessary in the initial stages of his training. If misdeeds persist after the age of about three months, when he should be gaining control of his bladder, one should try to catch him 'in the act', and at once scold him and remove him to his regular spot in the garden. *It is useless to scold and punish him after the event*, as he will not understand what he has done to displease. St Bernards are usually much easier to house-train than some of the smaller breeds, and in good weather, when doors can be left open, they should soon be naturally clean. If mishaps do occur on rugs and carpets, staining can be avoided by prompt washing with ammonia and water, or with soda water.

Bad habits are difficult to break, and a fully-grown St Bernard, weighing perhaps some fourteen stone, has to be kept under control, or he will be a constant source of worry to his owner. The family may know that when their pet jumps upon them in play, no harm is intended, but strangers (and indeed friends) will certainly not appreciate this type of behaviour. Most St Bernards are gentle and quiet by nature, once the boisterous puppy stage has passed, but one cannot stress too much that strict early training is absolutely essential. A puppy must learn the meaning of the word 'No', even if one has to smack him hard with a folded newspaper, or something rather more resilient, to get the message through to him. One should never punish unjustly, or when the punishment cannot be associated with the misdeed. Once a St Bernard learns that his physical strength is greater than that of the person in charge of him, there will be problems unless he has been taught obedience when young.

For lead training, a double choke chain collar, of the type illustrated, is recommended, as it can be used to check the puppy but will never pull tight enough to throttle him. It is a good plan to accustom him to the collar for a few days, first without, and then with, the lead attached, before encouraging him to walk beside you while you hold the lead. Encourage him to follow you by rewarding him with titbits, and make the early lessons very brief, so that he does not become bored.

It is most important to train a puppy to return to you when called, and this is easy if you begin soon enough. Make the lessons fun, with titbits and plenty of praise. We were once asked to help the owner of a very large St Bernard dog, who had been acquired as an adult after inadequate early training. He was gentle and affectionate, but had one fault; he would not return when called. She had been advised to attach a long length of rope to his collar, with which to pull him back when he disobeyed. In order to give him plenty of freedom, she purchased a 25-yard length, wrapped and tied it round her waist, and set out. Bruno had his play, but, when it was time to return home, she called, and hauled on the rope in vain. She was eventually taken for a 5-mile

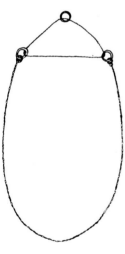

Double-choke chain collar, can never be pulled so tight as to throttle the dog.

canter, which only ceased when she succeeded in winding herself and the rope round a tree and shouting for help.

If training proves a problem, it may, as a last resort, be helpful to take the puppy to some of the excellent dog-training classes which are often available, especially in urban areas. Here the dog will not only receive lessons in elementary obedience, and be taught to walk at heel without pulling, sit on command etc., but will grow accustomed to the proximity of strangers and other dogs. The addresses of suitable training organisations can be obtained on application to the Kennel Club.

Inoculation

A puppy cannot be inoculated against distemper, hard-pad, leptros-pirosis, and hepatitis until he is eleven or twelve weeks old. Until he has been immunised, it is most important that he is not allowed to come in contact with other dogs, or visit places where they have been, such as pavements and parks. Each year he will need a booster injection. Should you at any time wish to place your St Bernard in a reputable boarding kennel, it will be necessary to produce his vaccination certificate.

Feeding

When you collect your puppy, the breeder should supply you with a diet sheet, giving precise instructions as to how he should be fed. It is most important to follow these instructions carefully in order to give the least possible disruption to the accustomed routine. During the first day or two, it is wise to feed a new puppy very sparingly, to minimise the risk of a digestive upset, due to change of food and water. The importance of correct feeding during the growing stages cannot be too strongly emphasised, and it is desirable for one member of the family to be responsible for this, rather than it being delegated to anyone who happens to have an appropriate moment to spare.

All breeders have their own recipes for successful puppy rearing, and few agree, but the following is our suggestion for an eight-week-old St Bernard puppy. The quantities given are approximate, as all puppies are individuals, and one must use one's common sense, according to the puppy's weight and general development.

Breakfast

One pint (600 ml) of warm milk, into which is beaten a raw egg yoke, and two tablespoonful of baby cereal such as Farex or Farlene. Never give cow's milk, as this can make the bowels too loose. Goats' milk, or proprietary baby milk such as Ostermilk, is ideal, or Lactol, which can be purchased from most good pet shops. Some chemists will sell out-of-date baby foods and milk (which are quite suitable for puppy feeding) at a reduced price. We use B. O. C. M. Gold Top Calf Milk, which is available from corn merchants.

Lunch

Three-quarters of a pound (340 g) of raw minced meat, mixed with 2-3 oz (50-70 g) of Puppy or Terrier Biscuite. Over this should be sprinkled a heaped teaspoonful of feeding bone flour. This is a special product, containing calcium and other minerals, and is not the type one puts on roses! It can be obtained from some vets or, postally, from Messrs Dunlops, 16 St Michaels Street, Dumfries.

Tea

One pint of milk.

Supper

Repeat lunch, omitting bone flour, but adding a few drops of cod-liver oil. If this meal is given late in the evening, before the owners go to bed themselves, it will help to settle the puppy down contentedly for the night.

Quantities of food must be increased as the puppy grows, and the bone flour stepped up gradually to a dessertspoonful. At the age of three months the milk feed at teatime can be discontinued. Breakfast cereals, such as Ready Brek and Weetabix, can gradually replace the baby cereal, and cow's milk can slowly be introduced. Variety can be achieved by occasionally giving fish or tinned dog meat instead of mince. At six months the puppy should be having two meals daily, with about 3 lb (1.4 kg) of meat and 1½ lb (700 g) of biscuit in each. An adult St Bernard needs about 5 lb (2.2 kg) of meat and 1½ lb of biscuit daily, but this is only approximate; a very active dog needs more food than a lethargic one. One must feed according to individual condition, and not allow the animal to get too fat. A fat, over-weight St Bernard is not a healthy one, and will not live to a ripe old age. Any tendency to over-weight should mean a cut in the biscuit ration, and the meat, too, if necessary. Bone flour should be given until the dog is at least eighteen months old, and a weekly dose of this and cod-liver oil will help to keep your pet in good health throughout life.

In order to save costs, many breeders feed paunch and offal, which is sometimes obtainable from local abbatoirs. Paunch is the uncooked stomach of a bullock or sheep, the former being the most nutritious. It is not a pleasant food to handle, but is the most economical method of feeding a large dog. Schools of thought vary as to whether it should be

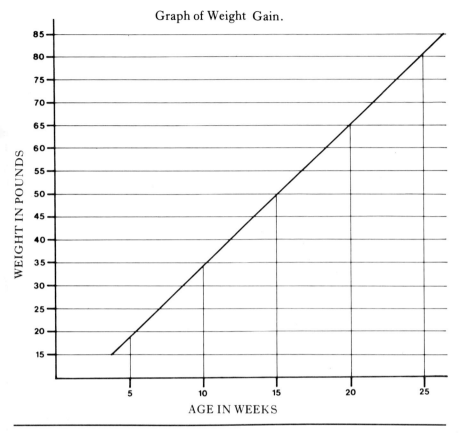

Graph of Weight Gain.

Age (months)	Average Height (inches)	
	DOG	BITCH
4	20	19
5	23	22
6	26	25
7	27	26
8	28	27
9	29	28
12	31-33	28-30

Average height at given ages.

Measurements must be taken at the top of the shoulder blades: the common fault is to take the measurement too far up the neck. Very forward puppies can easily exceed the above measurements

given raw or cooked. Raw paunch, containing the remains of grass, is a wonderful source of vitamins, but can cause tape-worm infection. Cooking reduces the calorie value, in any case less than that of meat, and results in a most unpleasant aroma unless a pressure cooker is available. It is probably wise to feed it raw and to be on the look-out for tapeworm segments in the motions. About 6 lb (2.7 kg) of paunch daily should satisfy an adult St Bernard. Other good supplements to the diet are hearts, bullocks' throats, and udders, all of which should be cooked. Liver is much appreciated, but should be fed very sparingly; it is most useful for tickling the appetite of an indifferent feeder. Tinned dog foods are occasionally a standby, but should not form the main source of a St Bernard's diet (apart from being very expensive); they are invaluable if taking a dog away on holiday, but unless fed in moderation, and mixed with plenty of biscuit, they can upset the bowels if a dog is unused to them. The modern 'complete' dog foods are not an economical way of feeding a St Bernard, and we are of the opinion that animals fed exclusively on them tend to lack resistance to infection.

Green vegetables, grated carrots, and cooked onions are a most valuable source of vitamins in the diet, and the latter are especially beneficial if there is any tendency to skin troubles. Potatoes should never be given.

Large hard biscuits are a good way of cleaning the teeth, and are much enjoyed. Bones also help in this respect, but only large marrow bones should be permitted, as these cannot splinter. Too many bones can cause constipation. Not long ago, we found Cassie, a beautiful 5-month-old bitch puppy, dead in her kennel one morning. A post mortem revealed that a bone splinter had pierced the bowel, causing internal bleeding. She had been in the habit of raiding the dustbin. Beware!

The St Bernard who does not relish his food and finish it all up in a few moments is a rarity, but should a puppy fail to clear his dish, on no account should the leavings be left for him to eat when it suits his pleasure. What is left should be removed, and a reduced quantity given at the next feed. At about three months, some puppies get tired of milky feeds, and in this case they should be omitted, and the other meals increased in quantity. This is the time to start introducing more variety into the diet.

Never allow a St Bernard to be given titbits from the family meal table, or he may feel it is his right to help himself when you are not present! Strict early training in this respect is essential before he grows so much that his nose is at table level. It has been known for a St Bernard to acquire the knack of knocking food off the table with his tail, and catching it before it reaches the floor!

Sleeping Accommodation

It is useless to provide a young puppy with a wicker dog basket, as this will only be chewed to pieces. The best solution is a thick washable blanket, placed in the position where it is desirable for the puppy to sleep. His first night alone in his new sleeping quarters will probably prove disturbing for all the household, but one should, if possible, turn a deaf ear to his melancholy howling. Once you weaken and allow him to be brought upstairs to the bedroom with you, he will naturally expect the same privilege on subsequent occasions, and the first battle for obedience will have been lost. During his first few nights on his own, a stone hot-water bottle, well wrapped in a blanket, may prove a comfort, and the sound of a radio may also help to ease his loneliness. He can, of course, have his own toys, provided these are of a size that cannot be swallowed. Small rubber balls are highly dangerous, as they can so easily become wedged in the throat. An old soft leather slipper is usually a great favourite.

Many adult St Bernards like to sleep stretched up on their sides, or even on their backs, so no basket is ever ultimately large enough. Usually, they dislike the heat, possibly because they originated in a cold country, and often prefer to lie on a cold, tiled floor rather than on a carpet or blanket. If you have the space, an old mattress in a washable cover, or even an old settee, makes an ideal bed for an adult St Bernard.

Like all puppies, St Bernards spend a large part of the day asleep, and should be allowed to rest peacefully. Children in the family must be made to understand that the new puppy needs his sleep as much as they do, and should not be constantly disturbed. They should never be allowed to pick the puppy up, as so much harm can be caused if this is done incorrectly. When carrying a small puppy, always place one hand under its rear end to support its weight, rather than dangling it in the air by holding both hands under its armpits.

Exercise

St Bernards do not need a great deal of exercise. An adult dog will get almost all he needs if he has a large garden to roam in. Failing this, about twenty minutes' run, twice daily, preferably off the lead, will keep him in good condition. In hot weather, one should always give exercise in the cool of the early morning, and during the evening, rather than during the hottest part of the day.

It is very important not to over-exercise a St Bernard puppy. Until he is six months old, walks outside the house and garden should not be attempted. Owing to the very rapid weight increase made by puppies of this breed, it is most unwise to put too much strain on the legs at an early age. One must start with short periods of exercise, and let the muscles build up gradually. The puppy should be watched carefully for any signs of tiring. From puppyhood to about a year old, many St Bernards go through a most ungainly growing stage, when they may appear loose-limbed, and unsound in movement. As the muscles develop this phase usually passes, if one is patient, does not over-exercise, and does not let the puppy become too fat.

Owing to their great weight, St Bernard puppies should not be encouraged to play boisterously, as they can so easily fall awkwardly and damage tendons and ligaments. During the long time these take to heal, permanent deformation of other limbs may occur, owing to the weight being abnormally distributed when the puppy moves. If there are children in the family it is often difficult to avoid rough play, but when the puppy is young, it must be allowed the long periods of rest it needs.

Grooming

Daily attention with a stiff brush is necessary to keep a St Bernard's coat free from tangles, and to remove loose hair. Special attention must always be paid to the areas behind the ears, and to the longer hair at the back of the hind legs, where knots tend to form. The hair on the tail also tends to get matted, and should be well brushed rather than combed, or it may develop a ragged appearance. Smooth St Bernards can best be groomed with a hound glove. St Bernards cast their coats about every six months, and at these times the daily grooming is of extra importance.

During regular grooming sessions it is important to keep a sharp look out for fleas and lice, which even the best-cared-for dogs can catch during exercise, or when taken to a show. During the summer months, keep a wary eye open for harvest mites between the toes, which can cause intense irritation and incessant nibbling of the feet. More information on these parasites will be found in Chapter 15.

Various proprietary coat dressings on the market are of assistance during grooming, and their regular use will help to impart a healthy shine to the coat.

Should it be necessary to bath a St Bernard, an old, flat-bottomed, metal bungalow-bath is ideal for the purpose. Baths of this type can often be obtained from junk shops. A good insecticidal shampoo, such as J. D. S., is recommended, and can easily be rinsed from the coat with a hose attached to a warm-water tap. Always choose a warm day for the operation, and allow the dog to dry off afterwards in a warm place. Thorough drying is always essential not only after bathing, but after exercise in wet weather.

The eyes should be washed occasionally with warm water, especially if there is any tendency to discharge. Ears need regular cleaning, and a few drops of olive oil, left in them overnight, will soften accumulated matter which can then be gently removed without probing.

If a St Bernard is reasonably active, his toe-nails should not need attention, but should they grow too long, trimming with clippers may be needed. This should be painless if one is careful not to cut back too far at a time. One does require a strong hand for this job, and if the dog is not co-operative it may be a task for the vet. Dew-claws are always likely to be a source of trouble, and most breeders remove them during the first week of life. Not only can they cause injury by catching and tearing, but are inclined to grow round like rams' horns and penetrate the flesh. To avoid this, they should be clipped periodically.

Kennelling

Every St Bernard prefers to be treated as a family dog, and his best kennel is therefore the home of his owner. However, there is a limit to the number of dogs that can be accommodated in the house, and if one intends to keep more than two or three Saints, or two of mixed sex, it will be necessary to plan some kennels. On some occasions it is inconvenient to have even the most domesticated and well-behaved St Bernard in the house, and it is probably a good plan to accustom a puppy to spending short periods in outside accommodation, so that he will not resent having occasionally to be banished from the house.

If the proposed kennelling is very extensive, planning permission from the local authority may be required, so it is wise to check on this, and on the attitude of neighbours who may be disturbed by noise.

Kennels should be situated as near the house as possible, so that the dogs can be kept under observation and will have the interest of watching family comings and goings. Converted stables and out-houses make ideal accommodation for St Bernards, provided they are airy, light, and not damp; if these are not available, brick-built or breeze block structures are preferable to wooden sheds. If wood is used, the kennels must be insulated, and the inner surfaces lined with zinc sheeting, as a determined St Bernard can chew his way through boarding in a matter of minutes. The kennels should be of adequate size, with spacious runs, in which there is shade in summer.

Run surfaces for St Bernards must be concreted or covered with slabbing, or they will soon become mud-patches in winter. There should be a good slope away from the kennel for drainage. Covered runs, for exercise during wet weather are a great asset. Kennel floors can be wood, or insulated concrete, and the dogs must be provided with sleeping beds, which can be either wooden benches raised from the floor, or boxed structures in which they can lie full-length. Wood shavings make ideal bedding, and are preferable to straw, from which dogs can become infected with parasites, and fungal organisms.

It is most important that kennels and runs should be secure and totally escape-proof, so all latches should be of the type that defeats even the intelligence of a Saint. Strong bolts on the outsides of doors are more satisfactory than catches and other gadgets. Runs should be constructed of good quality weld-mesh, as dogs can climb up chain-link fencing, and chicken wire is obviously not tough enough for St Bernards. They should be *at least* 6 ft high. Aluminium posts, such as old scaffolding poles, make good supports, and the weld-mesh can be easily attached to it with hook-bolts.

Apart from puppies and the very elderly, St Bernards will only appreciate heat in the coldest weather. Infra-red strip heaters, suspended from kennel ceilings, are the most satisfactory sources of warmth, but these should be properly installed, and should be at least eight feet above the ground, with all the wiring well out of the dogs' reach. In low wooden kennels they are most unsafe, as are any forms of portable paraffin heaters. Fire extinguishers should always be to hand.

The dogs will require a liberal supply of fresh water. Automatic drinkers of the self-flushing type are ideal, providing the piping is not plastic. Failing these the best solution is probably large metal buckets, slotting into metal rings on the walls, as these can be quickly removed for cleaning. Large porcelain sinks cannot be upset, but they are cumbersome to empty and keep clean.

If it is intended to keep more than a few dogs, a kennel kitchen will be needed. A sink with hot and cold water is essential here, in addition to cooking facilities, electric mincer, refrigerator, and freezer. Large metal dustbins make good vermin-proof stores for dry foods. Walls should preferably be tiled, and working surfaces covered with easily-cleaned material.

Dogs are happiest living in pairs, so two bitches may be housed together, or a dog kennelled with a bitch. Two stud dogs, however, may not always agree. It is necessary to have separate accommodation for in-season bitches, and whelping bitches, as far away from the main kennels as possible.

Provided the St Bernard's quarters are secure, dry, draught-proof, and clean, he should be reasonably content in them. If it can be arranged, it is a good plan to give each dog an occasional turn in the house, as this helps to develop the intelligence, and gets the dog used to being handled and meeting strangers.

13 Showing Your St Bernard

Dog showing can be tremendous fun, except when taken too seriously and allowed to become a grim matter of life and death. If you cannot lose with a good grace, you should not show dogs!

All British shows are held under the jurisdiction of the Kennel Club, which has its offices in Clarges Street, Piccadilly, London W1. A dog must be registered at the Kennel Club in the name of the latest owner before it can be exhibited. The various types of show are as follows.

Exemption shows

These are the smallest shows, but there is no separate classification for individual breeds. Four classes are allowed for pedigree dogs, and there are usually others for cross-breds, and also several novelty classes, such as 'The dog most like its owner'. These shows are usually held during the summer months, in conjunction with fêtes and other charity events.

These are the only shows where Kennel Club registration is not compulsory, and where pedigree and non-pedigree dogs can be shown together. Entries are made at the show, and not in advance, as at other shows. Exemption shows are excellent training grounds for puppies, accustoming them to the atmosphere of the show ring and the proximity of other dogs.

Sanction shows

These are small shows of not more than 25 classes and are often held at evenings and weekends. Only members of the promoting society may compete, but membership is usually open to anyone who pays the small joining subscription. Challenge Certificate winners, and certain other categories of winning dogs, may not compete, so they are good shows for novice dogs and owners. Usually the classes are all open to 'Any Variety' of dog, so the competition may be keen. No benches are provided for the dogs to sit in to be viewed by the public.

Limited shows

These are similar to Sanction shows, but the standard is a little higher, and more classes are provided. Separate classes are usually available for a few breeds, but only rarely for St Bernards. Again, one must be a member of the promoting society in order to compete. Challenge Certificate winners are not eligible, and the shows are usually unbenched.

Open Shows
At these shows there are no restrictions on the number of classes, which are open to all, whether members or not. Occasionally there are breed classes for St Bernards, and the shows are sometimes benched. These are usually 'all-day' shows, commencing in mid-morning. The time that dogs may be removed is printed in the schedule and is usually strictly enforced. At all-benched shows, dogs must remain on their benches except when being shown or exercised. Champions are often entered in the Open classes at these shows, and the standard may be very high.

Championship Shows
These are the 'Classic Events' of the dog-show world. About 30 are held annually, in various parts of the country. The most famous is Cruft's, at present held in London, under the management of the Kennel Club. The Championship shows are so called because only at these events can a dog win the awards which he needs to become a Champion; these are the coveted Challenge Certificates awarded to the Best Dog and Best Bitch in most of the different breeds. A dog must be awarded three of these Challenge Certificates, under three different judges, to qualify for the honour of putting Champion in front of its name. If one wishes to make one's dog a Champion, it may be necessary to travel all over the country to do so, possibly from Edinburgh in the north, to Paignton in the south.

Entry fees at shows may vary between 30 pence per class at a Sanction show, to £6 to £9 at one of the major Championship events. The larger shows are expensive to run, as the summer outdoor events require huge marquees for benching dogs, and must provide covered judging rings in case of rain. For winter shows, expensive halls must be hired. Printing, benching, postage, and judges' expenses are also major items, and costs are rising annually. Prize money, if any, is insignificant, and has not been increased during the last decade to match the great escalation of entry fees.

Puppies under 6 months of age are not eligible for exhibition at any show held under Kennel Club rules. St Bernard puppies are not, in any case, mature enough to be taken to shows at this age. If you have a promising puppy, it is better to wait until he is almost a year old before showing him, as he will be a vastly improved dog when he has muscled up and matured in head.

Details of forthcoming shows are published weekly in the advertisement sections of the canine magazines *Dog World* and *Our Dogs*, together with the addresses from which schedules and entry forms can be obtained. Before completing an entry form, you should closely study the definitiions of the various classes, as if you enter in the wrong class you will later be disqualified. Classes for St Bernards alone are something of a rarity, except at the Championship Shows, but sometimes there may be classes for all dogs in the Working Group, or for Large Breeds, for both of which a St Bernard would be eligible. At some shows a 'Special Beginners' class is scheduled to give newcomers a chance, but the definition should be carefully checked, as it varies from show to show. If entering a young dog for the first time, it is wise to try one's luck in the lower classes, rather than to be too ambitious. One or two classes is sufficient for a dog's first appearance, as a youngster may so easily become bored standing in the ring for a long period, and this may prejudice him against shows at the start of his career.

A dog show is a beauty contest, and to stand any chance in keen competition, it is essential that one's exhibit should be looking his (or her) very best, and be trained to show his charms to advantage. The dog should be regularly groomed during the period before the show, to stimulate the circulation and improve the condition of the coat. If necessary, on the day before the show, he should be bathed all over, or have his tail, legs, chest, and underparts well washed. Too much washing can make a coat 'blow', especially if the dog is nearing the moult. His ears should be cleaned, and any unsightly loose hair plucked (but *never* cut) from the outside of the ear flaps and between the toes. If he had been groomed well in the preceding weeks, there should be no matts in the coat, but it is wise to check the long hair on the thighs, tail and behind the ears. The nails should not need trimming if the dog has been adequately exercised.

Your dog's show training can begin when he is only a puppy. It is most important that the person who is to handle him in the ring has him under complete control, as if he misbehaves, and upsets other exhibits, their owners will not be pleased, and neither will your chances of being amongst the winners be enhanced. It should be emphasised here that no bad-tempered dog, who would fortunately be a rarity in this breed, should be taken anywhere near a show. Should a dog bite the judge, another exhibitor, or fellow exhibit, you will be reported to the Kennel Club, and the dog will probably be banned from future shows. At a benched show, spectators, especially children, always fall in love with the St Bernards, and try to stroke them, so to take a dog of uncertain temperament to a dog show is just asking for trouble.

If you have trained your dog properly as a puppy, he should be well

used to walking on a lead without pulling, but before taking him to a
show get him used to walking up and down on a loose lead at an easy
pace. You must also teach him to stand sideways for several minutes
without moving, as he will need to do this while the judge is making his
assessment. He should be accustomed to having his lips gently lifted to
reveal his bite, so that he does not protest when the judge checks this
important point. If, before entering a show, you can manage to attend
one just as a spectator, you will learn much about the routine, and
understand what is expected of the dogs.

If getting to the show involves a car journey, the dog should be
accustomed to car travel beforehand. Most St Bernards love cars, and
this seldom proves a problem; in fact many will jump eagerly into any
car with the door left open, which can sometimes be embarrassing. If a
dog is nervous in the car, he may be car-sick, which you will not
appreciate if you have spent hours washing him beforehand, so if there
is any uncertainty, do not feed him before travelling and give him a
'Sealeg' tablet of the type used for sea-sickness.

Before setting off for the show you will need to assemble much
luggage for yourself and the dog. In addition to the collar and the lead
you intend to use in the ring, a strong chain will be necessary to fasten
your exhibit to the bench, and a rug for him to lie on. Some show
benches are horribly grubby, so you may like to take a cloth and some
mild disinfectant along with you as well. For an all-day event, a
drinking bowl will be necessary, some food for yourself, and a meal of
his favourite food for your Saint. He will have earned it before the day
is done! You must, of course, not forget the grooming equipment, and
some powder to clean his legs and underparts if he gets wet and
muddy; a large clean towel is always useful.

A few days before the larger shows, exhibitors receive passes and car
park tickets, which must not be forgotten in the last-minute rush, and
one should always remember to pack the show schedule in case of any
query. A clip to fasten one's ring number is important, and do not
forget the Aspirins for yourself: you will probably need them!

SHOW DAY
It is wise to set out for the show in good time so that you can find a
handy parking space for the car, and locate the bench where the dog
must sit, without getting flustered. Nothing is worse than trying to
struggle through a large crowded showground with a St Bernard and all
the aforementioned gear, when you know you are late and your class is
due to enter the ring. Almost equally as harassing is trying to find the
money to buy a show catalogue when you are clutching dog and gear!

Benches for St Bernards are usually far too small and unsteady for
the size of the dog, so an unseasoned exhibit may, justifiably, object to

the confinement and try to escape. Once when taking several dogs to a show without help, we had to leave one alone on his bench when returning to the car for the others, and were met at the entrance by the youngster, with a large portion of his bench dragging behind him on the end of his chain. We once had another almost throttled when he fell off the bench backwards; so it pays to be very careful, and never to leave your dog alone even for a minute until you are sure he settled down and grown accustomed to his surroundings.

It is important to find out as soon as possible at what time your class is likely to be judged; if it is one of the later ones, delay your final grooming of the dog until shortly before he is due to go in the ring. If the weather is hot and he tends to drool, tie a bib or towel round his neck to keep his dewlap dry.

When your class is called, take the dog into the ring, collect your ring number from the steward, and pin it to your person with the ring-clip. Always try to be calm and confident, even though your knees may be knocking; dogs soon sense any tenseness on the part of their handlers, and may be unsettled in consequence. If showing for the first time, it is wise to place oneself well along the line of waiting exhibitors, so that one can copy the procedure of those more experienced. While standing in the ring, never allow your dog to interfere with that of another exhibitor.

JUDGING PROCEDURE
When all the exhibits in the class are assembled, the steward will tell the judge that all is ready for him. Many judges ask all the exhibitors in a class to go round the ring together in a circle, before the dogs are examined individually. This gives the dogs a chance to settle down, and the judge an opportunity for a quick overall survey. The normal method is then for the judge to call each exhibit in turn into the centre of the ring, examine it thoroughly, or not so thoroughly, and then ask the handler to move it, either in a straight line up and down, or in a triangle. It is so important to concentrate all your attention on your dog, and to listen carefully to the judge's questions and instructions. He will probably ask the age of the dog, and if so, you should volunteer simply this information, and not launch into a description of his whole life story or the prizes he won last week at Blanktown Exemption Show! The judge may ask you to move the dog in such a way that he can observe its sideways movement, and in this case you must be sure not to place yourself between dog and judge, however good your own movement may be.

Once the judge has completed his appraisal, the handler should take his place again in the line, while the rest of the dogs are examined. Once all have been seen, most judges come down the line again, making a final comparison of the exhibits, and this is the moment when you must have your dog standing sideways-on to the judge, and looking his absolute best. See he is standing squarely on all four legs, with his head held slightly up; some exhibitors 'string up' their dogs at this point, by moving the collar up tightly behind the ears and stretching the head and neck upwards, which makes the back appear much shorter. If you have not practised this, it is best not to attempt it, as you may upset your dog when trying it for the first time.

If you concentrate on your dog and the instructions of the judge, you will forget to feel nervous, and be ready to obey any final instruction. You may be asked to move your dog a second time, if the judge wishes to compare its movement with that of another; there is an old adage among the judges, 'when in doubt – move them about', so always be on the alert to obey any instruction promptly.

When the judge has made his mind up, he will beckon the winners, or those from whom he intends to select his winners, into the centre of

Miss M. Hindes's Ch. Burtonswood Black Tarquin, winner of 12 Challenge Certificates, and Best in Show at the first English St Bernard Championship Show in 1979.

the ring. If you are among the lucky ones, move at once to the position indicated, but never relax until the judge has marked his book, in case he changes his mind at the last minute.

At the end of the class always make a fuss of your dog, and let him know he has pleased you, so that he will learn to think of a show as a happy occasion. Always try to accept defeat with a good grace. There is always another show – and another judge!

If a dog wins his class, and is not beaten in a subsequent class, he will be required to enter the ring again later, to compete with other unbeaten dogs for the Best of Sex award, which at a Championship show, will be a Challenge Certificate. The two Challenge Certificate winners then compete for the Best of Breed award. At the end of the show, the winning St Bernard must meet the other Best of Breed winners among the Working breeds, to determine the Best in the Working Group. This winner then challenges the winners of the other five groups for the award of Best in Show. To achieve this at a

A winning St Bernard from Scotland. Mr and Mrs R. Gardner's Ch. Laird O'Glayva of Treeburn 1984.

Championship show is every exhibitor's dream, but is an ambition realised by only a few.

Once the judging is over, you should return your dog to his bench, and give him a drink, and possibly food. He will then settle down and rest until it is time to leave for home. Most of the bigger shows have a strictly enforced removal time, so if you have been judged in the morning, there can be quite a long wait. This is the time to get acquainted with other exhibitors, who will then have time to talk and answer your questions. Most judges, if they have courage, and confidence in their judgement, go round the benches after the judging, so you may have an opportunity to ask for an opinion of your dog. Always remember, even if you were among the losers, that everyone is entitled to their own opinion, and not all judges think alike, or attach the same importance to various parts of the Standard. If they did, there would be no point in holding dog shows!

14 Judging

At one time, it was customary to serve an apprenticeship of several years as a breeder and exhibitor before being invited to judge St Bernards. Today, this is not always the case, as owing to an increase in the number of shows scheduling classes for the breed there appears to be a dearth of specialist judges. One may therefore be asked to officiate in the ring at an Open show after only brief experience as an exhibitor, and possibly none as a breeder.

To judge well requires confidence, which only comes with a belief in the adequacy of one's knowledge coupled with a calm, fearless and unbiased approach to the task. If these essential attributes are lacking, it is as well to decline a judging invitation. Bad judging, whether resulting from incompetence, or the hope of reciprocal favours, does a disservice to the breed: in many cases, the winners of today become the parents of tomorrow, so faults which should have been severely penalised in the ring are perpetuated.

However great your justification for confidence, when judging for the first time you will probably realise how little you really know. This is nothing to be ashamed of, and should lead to even greater analysis of the breed and its Standard. The bad judges are often the ones who think they know it all, and are not prepared to study the finer points of breed structure.

When entering the ring for the first time, most new judges feel some sense of apprehension, but this should soon be overcome with the deep interest felt when examining the dogs. This same concentration on the task in hand should also make one deaf to the often intentionally audible remarks of ringside critics, many of whom have never judged in their lives.

On the auspicious occasion of one's first judging appointment, it is wise to leave for the show in good time, as a calm and unflurried arrival is essential. Be suitably dressed in comfortable clothes for the task ahead, as much bending and stooping will be necessary; tight, short skirts for lady judges may prove embarassing, as however alluring the view of one's thighs, it is the legs of the dogs the ringsiders have come to see. Dangling jewellery may disturb the dogs, and likewise unfastened ties: a lady in another breed was almost strangled when a dog grasped her flowing red scarf having mistaken it for a piece of meat. It is a good plan to take a towel to wipe one's hand after examining each exhibit, as, although this should be provided, it often is not.

Early arrival at the show allows ample time to collect one's judging book from the show secretary, and assemble one's thoughts for the task that lies ahead. It is very bad manners to keep exhibitors waiting, when they and their dogs are keyed up to go into the ring. One should introduce oneself to the ring steward, whose task it is to collect and marshal the dogs in each class. Tell him how you would like the dogs arranged in the ring, and if in doubt ask him to explain to you how the judging book should be marked.

If the ring is large enough, it is a good plan to ask all the exhibitors to move their dogs twice round the ring at the beginning of each class, to give them a chance to settle down, and so that brief preliminary appraisal can be made. When examining the dogs individually, make a careful assessment of the overall picture, before going carefully over the individual points. Always be gentle, especially when handling the mouth: many a good puppy has been unnecessarily frightened by the pummelling received from a heavy-handed judge. When moving the dogs, it is a good plan to let them gait in a triangle, so that you can study the action both coming and going, and also from the side, without moving your own position. Watch them as they turn the corners, as when they are 'out of stride' unsoundness is often easy to detect. Vicious temperament in St Bernards should always be ruthlessly penalised, but one can forgive nervousness, especially in puppies. A dog which refuses to do himself justice when moving can always be given a second chance after the other exhibits have been examined, as he will sometimes overcome his fear on the second occasion.

When judging it is always necessary to take handling into consideration; good skilful presentation can enhance the chances of an indifferent dog, while a fine specimen can be handicapped if shown by a novice. A novice judge should always be on the look-out for the tricks of seasoned and wily exhibitors: always be suspicious of the dog moved in such a way that his movement cannot be properly assessed, and ask the handler, if necessary, to take him again at a slow pace. The handler who opens his dog's mouth himself, giving only a fleeting glimpse of the bite to the judge, could be trying to hide a badly undershot jaw, or even no teeth at all. Many a handler's knee has propped up a St Bernard backend with a tendency to collapse. The tale is told of a Saint bitch who scraped her flank on a sheet of tin the night before a show, removing a large patch of skin and hair; a carefully constituted patch of hair was affixed to the wound, and, with the other side turned towards the judge, she won the C. C.

St Bernards do not often attract such large classes that there is insufficient time to thoroughly examine each exhibit, and one should give equal attention to all the dogs in the class, irrespective of whether they are likely to be among the winners or not. All have paid the same high entry fee, and entered their dogs for your opinion, and after the judging you should be able to give an assessment of every dog, whether winner or loser.

It is most important when judging to have a clear picture of one's ideal Saint fixed in the mind, and to compare each exhibit with this ideal. Always judge the virtues, rather than the faults. For those watching from the ringside, it is often possible to appraise the priorities and competence of a judge by the way he uses his hands. One can sense the appreciation of a well-shaped skull, strong muzzle, good shoulder placement, well-boned legs, good feet, level topline etc. There is nothing more irritating than the judge who moves all the exhibits so much that they and their handlers are exhausted, and then places the unsound movers at the top of the line!

One should be firm and definite in making decisions, and not be influenced by personal considerations, or the past records of the dogs being shown; if a well-known winner does not come up to expectations, and you can fault it, or it is not looking its best, do not be influenced by what other judges have done in the past. Everyone will attach different degrees of importance to various faults and virtues, and no two judges' evaluation is the same. Judging can lose you friends, but they will not be the ones worth having. Dogs bred by oneself should be judged as objectively as all the rest. If they deserve to be placed, they must go up, even though the uncharitable will say you have favoured your own breeding.

When all the dogs have been examined, if the class is large, or the ring small, it is best to select those from which the final placings will be made, and allow the rest to leave the ring. This allows more space for the final and most important assessment. Try not to be hesistant in making the final placings, as changing one's mind indicates indecision, and can lead to mistakes.

After the judging, one should, if asked, be able to give reasons for placing or not placing an exhibit, but one should never feel the need to apologise for putting a dog down. One will be asked to write a report on the winners for publication in the canine press, and it is a courtesy to exhibitors to do this as fully as possible.

When experience has been gained in judging breed classes at Open show level, the next hurdle is graduation to Championship show judging. Before approval by the Kennel Club to award Challenge Certificates is granted, the aspiring judge must complete a questionnaire giving details of judging experience, together with a list of dogs from his kennels included in the Stud Book. This information is placed before the Judges' Sub-Committee, who will then decide on the new judge's suitability to judge at Championship show level.

When judging St Bernards thirty years ago, the technique was very different to that used today. It was customary for the exhibitors to stand shoulder to shoulder in the ring with their dogs between them, with just their heads showing towards the judge. Assessment was made almost entirely on the merits of the heads and fronts; the rest was hidden as much as possible! As a result of this concentration on head points to the exclusion of all else, movement and conformation were neglected, and the breed suffered in consequence. Happily, today, it is usual to judge the whole dog, and our breed can now compete on equal terms with other breeds in the Working Group.

Extracts from *The St Bernard Club Year Book*, 1913.

CHAMPION.
The Pride of Sussex.

The Property of Mr. H. STOCKEN and Miss F. SAMUEL.
The best known St. Bernard of the day.

His record is marvellous. He has won 23 Challenge Certificates and The Brewers' Cup at Birmingham for best St. Bernard or Mastiff three years in succession, besides also having won the Prize for the Best Sporting or Non-Sporting Dog or Bitch of any breed at Birmingham and Crufts.

AT STUD, FEE £5 5s. 0d.

SIRE of VALINTINE NI TOUCHE, Pup weighing 184 lbs. at 12 months.

ALSO AT STUD :—

DON OF SUSSEX by Ch. The Pride of Sussex,
(ROUGH)   ex. Gypsy of Sussex.
NERO OF SUSSEX by Ch. Country Swell, ex.
(SMOOTH)   Demure of Duffryn.
BRIERY OF SUSSEX, by Ch. Country Swell, ex.
                           Demure of Duffryn.
FEE for these three Dogs, £3 3s. 0d.

Further particulars apply—

H. Stocken, Court House, Copthorne, Sussex.

AT STUD.
CH. HENRY OF YARNTON

(b. March 23rd, 1912).

FULL CHAMPION AT AGE OF 18 MONTHS.

MOST TYPICAL SMOOTH OF THE DAY.

Brilliant orange colour, dense black head—shading; splendid bone; capital mover.

SIRING FIRST-CLASS STOCK.

Combines all the best strains of

CH. THE VIKING BLOOD,

which is doing most of the winning to-day.

FEE, to approved bitches, £5 5s. prepaid.

Apply—

Mrs. PARKER, Yarnton, Oxford.

Station YARNTON, G.W.R.   Telegrams: "PARKER, YARNTON, KIDLINGTON."

15 Common Ailments

A St Bernard should have a reasonably long and trouble-free life, provided he is sensibly fed, adequately exercised, and comfortably housed. Above all, he should not be allowed to get too fat, as an over-weight dog will not be a healthy one, nor is he likely to make 'old bones'.

A vigilant owner will soon notice if a dog is off-colour and listless, and will investigate the cause. The temperature is one of the indications of the seriousness of any indisposition. Normally, when taken in the rectum, it is 38.6°C(101.5°F), but it can vary slightly. Should it exceed 39.2°(102.5°F), this should be regarded as a danger signal, and the reason should be determined. One should never delay in calling the vet if symptoms of ill-health persist.

DISORDERS OF THE ALIMENTARY TRACT

Diarrhoea. When this occurs in suckling puppies it is usually the result of an infection, and must be treated promptly, either by anti-biotic injection, or dosage with a Neobiotic pump, which will control the fluid losses and bacteria.

In adult Saints, an attack of diarrhoea is often due to unsuitable food, either given or scavenged from elsewhere. The sufferer should be put on a restricted and very light diet, and a meal of arrowroot gruel may prove helpful. A medicine containing Chlorodyne is often effective, but if the trouble persists, or the temperature rises the vet should be consulted, as an infection could be present.

Constipation. This should never be neglected, in case there is obstruction of the bowels. It can occur as a result of eating too many bones. A dessertspoonful of liquid paraffin may help to move the bowels, and the addition of grated raw carrot and shredded cabbage to the diet is recommended. If a dog is straining to pass a motion, an enema of warm soapy water will often remedy the situation.

Bloat. The symptoms of this highly dangerous condition are an abnormal swelling and hardening of the abdomen, and extreme distress. It is caused by a tortion (twisting) of the stomach or bowel, which blocks the passage of food, and allows gases to accumulate and inflate the tract. Often it occurs after the dog has eaten a large dry meal, followed by a great quantity of water. Prompt operative treatment is necessary, to prevent rupture of the inflated organ.

Anal gland obstruction. The ducts from the anal glands lead into the rectum just inside the anus; especially in older dogs, these may sometimes become clogged. The condition can be painful, and can result in the animal dragging its rear along the ground in a sitting position. If untreated, abscesses and infection may be set up within the glands. A vet will squeeze the glands, and release an evil smelling fluid, after which, treatment with antibiotics may bring about a cure. The addition of roughage to the diet will make the stools more bulky, and help to empty the glands naturally.

Gastritis. Inflammation of the stomach can result from eating putrid or unsuitable food. The dog will drink copiously, and then vomit up what has been drunk. He should be kept quiet and warm, and given a diet of milk and barley water. Water should be withheld, and, if the vomiting continues, the vet must be consulted.

DISORDERS OF THE URINARY TRACT

Cystitis. This is inflammation of the bladder, and may be due to cold, or to the formation of urinary deposits, which block the passage and prevent urination. It can sometimes happen if a dog of clean habits is shut up for too long and is unable to relieve himself. Symptoms are fullness of the abdomen, and straining to pass water, which may only be produced in drops, and may be highly coloured or blood-stained. The victim should be given a light meatless diet, and have barley water to drink in preference to plain water. If the trouble does not clear up quickly, veterinary attention is essential.

Nephritis. St Bernards may suffer from a number of diseases of the kidneys. In acute cases there will be total loss of appetite, lassitude, pain over the kidneys, and a rise in temperature. Chronic kidney trouble sometimes occurs in older dogs, and is characterised by abnormal thirst, often followed by vomiting, poor appetite, and loss of weight. The cause may be due to stones, leptospiral infection, heart disease, or degeneration of the kidney tissue in old age. Veterinary advice should be sought, and the dog kept on a light meatless diet.

DISORDERS OF BITCHES

Eclampsia. Sometimes known as milk fever, this may occur in bitches during the late stages of pregnancy, and also in nursing bitches. It is the result of a low level of calcium in the blood. The symptoms are excitability, unsteadiness, and eventually convulsions and collapse. It is a highly dangerous condition and must be remedied by immediate injections of soluble calcium, so no time must be lost in calling a vet.

Mastitis. This inflammation of the milk glands usually results from a bitch having too much milk, either because her puppies have been removed, or her litter's requirements are too small. It can also occur in one or more glands as a result of injury, or blockage of a teat. Abscesses may form in the glands, and soreness and swelling make sucking painful. The trouble is treated by antibiotics, and by drugs to reduce the milk flow.

Metritis. Inflammation of the womb may occur after the birth of puppies, and can result from the presence of a dead puppy, or a retained afterbirth. Less serious cases usually respond to antibiotics.

Pyometra. Like metritis, the symptoms of pyometra (pus in the womb) are distension of the abdomen, and a foul-smelling, dark brown discharge. There is often vomiting and excessive thirst. This condition is more common in older bitches, and in many cases hysterectomy, (removal of the womb), is necessary. This is not a dangerous operation and many bitches take on a new lease of life after it has been carried out. There may, however, be a tendency to put on weight, so the diet would require reduction.

False pregnancy. Whether a bitch has been mated or not, she will sometimes show all the symptoms of being in whelp, although not pregnant; there may be abdominal swelling, production of milk, and all the other signs of approaching labour, such as panting and bed-making. If the condition is severe, it may be necessary to give sedatives, and tablets to reduce the milk flow, but normally the symptoms clear up naturally within a few days. Bitches in this state can make ideal foster mothers. If there is a history of false pregnancies after each season, a bitch may ultimately have to be spayed.

RESPIRATORY DISORDERS:

Kennel cough. This virus infection affecting the throat and surrounding areas has become very common during recent years. The dog frequently 'clears its throat', especially during exercise and when excited. The condition usually responds quickly to treatment with antibiotics. Although it is a mild ailment, dogs suffering from kennel cough should not be taken to shows, where they can spread the infection to others.

Bronchitis. This usually commences with a cold, cough, and difficulty in breathing, and is more common in older dogs. The sufferer remains in a sitting position, and will wheeze and gasp for breath. The patient should be kept warm and fed on a light diet. Holding the head over a steaming bowl of hot water, to which a teaspoonful of Friar's Balsam has been added, and persuading the dog to inhale the vapour, will often ease the breathing. Over-weight Saints are more prone to bronchial troubles, so if your dog suffers, reduce his weight.

DISORDERS DUE TO PARASITES

Like all dogs, the St Bernard may become host to a variety of internal

and external parasites. Owners must be continually on the look out fo
such infestation, as owing to the size of the dog, eradication onc
parasites are established can be a major problem. Various species o
worm may live inside the body, and parasitic mites and insects ma
inhabit the skin. All can cause varying degrees of unthriftiness an
should be eliminated.

Roundworms. These can vary in length from 1 to 8 inches, an
develop from eggs picked up by mouth. They are common in puppies
who are frequently infected from the teats of the mother. If no
eradicated, their presence can cause obstruction of the intestines, an
damage to the gut wall; the lungs may also be damaged, and respirator
troubles ensue. Fortunately, roundworms are easily and safely elimi
nated the use of the vermifuge Coopane, which is obtainable from
veterinary surgeons, and can be given as early as 3 weeks of age. A
puppies should be wormed as a precautionary measure.

Tapeworms. These are rare in puppies but more common in adu
dogs, especially those fed on a diet of raw tripe, or infested with fleas
which may act as intermediate hosts. Country dogs, exercised i
fields where sheep have grazed may also become infected; fleas, sheep
cattle, rabbits, and hares, may all act as secondary hosts to variou
species of tapeworm, and can pass on the eggs to the dog. Th
tapeworms grow from its head, or scolex, which becomes embedded i
the wall of the intestine by hooks and suckers. Strings of flat, whit
segments develop from the head, and the whole worm may be severa
feet in length. The end segments, which are bags of eggs, becom
detached, and are passed out in the dogs' motions. Examination wi
reveal them as flat, white structures, about one third of an inch long
which may be seen to move. In bad cases of infestation, dried segment
can usually be observed attached to the hair in the vicinity of the anus
In dosing for tapeworm, it is essential that the entire worm, includin
the embedded scolex, be got rid of; if the head remains, another chai
of segments will develop from it in a very short space of time. It i
therefore essential to obtain a good vermifuge from a veterinar
surgeson, and to give the correct dose.

Fleas. The dog flea is larger than the human variety, dark brown i
colour, and rarely bites mankind. Fleas are most commonly found i
the area of the back in front of the tail, and over the loins. They bree
in the bedding, floor covering, and accumulations of dirt in kennels an
sleeping quarters. The best precaution against them is therefor
scrupulous cleanliness and careful incineration of all used beddin
material. A mildly infested dog may be treated with one of the variou
proprietary flea products on the market, but for serious cases bathing
with an insecticdal shampoo may be necessary.

Lice. Dogs can acquire lice if barley straw is used for bedding, and the re commonly found in the vicinity of the ears, and on the neck and egs. They breed on the body of the animal, and their eggs, known as its, remain attached to the hair. Their biting causes intense irritation, o any scratching, especially in young puppies which seem extra usceptible, should be carefully investigated. Adult insects can be killed with powders and insecticidal shampoos but it is necessary for reatment to be repeated two or three times to ensure destruction of ests which have hatched following the initial treatment.

Ticks. These are most commonly acquired during the summer months, f dogs are exercised in woods and fields where sheep and rodents have een. Ticks affix themselves to the skin of an animal and suck the lood, becoming much enlarged in the process. Before attempting to emove an attached tick, it is essential to loosen the hold of the mbedded mouthparts, as if these are left in the skin, an unpleasant ump will ensue. Dabbing the tick with ether or methylated spirit will ause it to relax its grip so that it can be pulled away in one piece. A ighted cigarette held against its body is said to have the same effect, ut this method is only for the steady-handed! Ticks in certain tropical ountries can infect dogs with the dreaded biliary fever, which may be atal within a few hours, but fortunately this danger is not present in Britain.

Harvest mites. These insects have the appearance of grains of red sand, nd are found in the autumn. They burrow under the skin, causing ntense irritation. They are mainly picked up from the ground between he toes, causing the dog to constantly lick and bite his paws. Repeated reatment with a good powdered insecticide or shampoo is the only nethod of treatment.

DISORDERS OF THE EARS

Canker. This is a term loosely used to describe inflammation of the ear assage, which may result from an accumulation of mites, foreign natter, wax, or excessive hair. Irritation causes the dog to shake the ar and hold his head on one side; constant scratching will aggravate he condition. There is often an obnoxious dark brown discharge which nay become very hard, and clog the ear passage completely. Before leaning the ear it is a good plan to soften the discharge with a tea-poonful of warm olive oil, left in the ear overnight. Matter may be wiped away with cotton wool, but any probing of the actual ear passage hould be most carefully and gently done and is a job for the vet. When he ear is dry and clean it should be dressed with a proprietary liquid uch as Otoryl, or with Benzyl Benzoate. Powders should be avoided, s they tend to clog the ear passage. During the summer months there s always a risk of grass seeds becoming embedded in the ear passages, nd their removal is a job for the vet.

Haematoa. This accumulation of blood and serum within the ear flap can result in a large swelling, which must be lanced at its lowest point When all the fluid has been removed, the wound should be treated with antibiotics. This condition may arise following a bruise or injury, and can also result from constant scratching of the ear flap.

DISORDERS OF THE EYES

Conjunctivitis. Inflammation of the membrane covering the eye can be caused by infection or irritants. It usually responds to treatment with good eye ointment.

Entropion. This condition is caused when the edge of the eyelid turns inward and the eyelashes rub and irritate the surface of the eye. If untreated, the cornea may be damaged and eventual blindness result. It is often the result of excessive skin above the eye, and can be treated surgically, but animals suffering from it should not be used for breeding.

Ectropion. In this condition the lower eyelid turns out, exposing too much haw, which often becomes red and inflamed. The English standard for St Bernards now calls for reasonably tight eyelids without excessive haw.

SKIN DISORDERS

Abscesses. An abscess is a painful swelling containing pus, and is usually the result of a bacterial infection. It can be treated with antibiotics and with warm poultices. Bathing with a warm solution of Epsom salts may help to bring the swelling to a head. If these treatments fail, the abscess may have to be lanced, and the wound kept open until no further matter escapes.

Eczema. This term covers various forms of skin irritation, but there are two main types of true eczema: the *dry* and the *wet*. In the *dry* type scaly and cracked inflamed patches appear, often inside the thighs, in the arm pits, and along the belly. The *wet* type, which is more commonly found on the face, ear flaps, and back, consists of small, wet, raw sores, which matt the hair and cause irritation; scratching aggravates the condition. Eczema is variously ascribed to dietary factors, fungal infections, and vitamin and mineral deficiencies. A dose of laxative, followed by a complete change of diet, will often help to clear up the condition, and the dog should receive plenty of green vegetables. Cooked onions mixed in the food are often most helpful. The hair should be clipped away from the infected areas, and the sores cleaned with warm water and cotton wool. They can then be treated with an eczema lotion such as Kurmange. An old fashioned remedy which has been known to succeed in stubborn cases is a mixture of lard and flowers of sulphur.

Mange. In the early stages, this condition resembles eczema, but it is highly contagious, and is due to the presence of parasitic mites which burrow under the skin. In *sarcoptic mange,* or *scabies,* the infection is superficial, though the irritation is severe. Small spots resembling flea bites can be seen, and the hair drops out in patches. Scratching and biting causes small sores and scabs. The *follicular* variety is more serious and fortunately rare, as the mites mitrate inside the body and the poisons absorbed can eventually cause death. If either form of mange is suspected, veterinary advice should be obtained at once.

Inter-digital cysts. If a dog constantly licks one of his feet, the pockets between the toes should be examined for the presence of swellings known as inter-digital cysts. These small abscesses may eventually cause lameness. They are usually set up when a foreign body, such as a particle of grit, becomes lodged between the toes and penetrates the skin. Holding the affected foot in a warm solution of Dettol or Epsom salts several times daily will usually bring about a cure, but in stubborn cases lancing may be necessary.

DISORDERS OF THE BONES AND JOINTS

Sprains. Because of their weight, St Bernards are particularly prone to injuries of joints, tendons and ligaments. Especially in the case of puppies, awkward falls during exercise and play can result in injuries which only time and rest will cure. The stifle joint is particularly affected, and if care is not taken, a sprain here may result in permanent lameness. Application of ice-cold compresses, and as much rest as possible, are the best hopes of bringing about a cure.

Swollen elbows. These are usually caused by an accumulation of fluid within the elbow joint, and are similar to the athlete's 'water on the knee' condition. They are caused by the dog throwing his full weight on the ground when lying down, and damaging the fluid capsule within the joint. Heavier Saints are more prone to this unsightly condition, which is likely to occur if kennel flooring is stone or concrete rather than wood. Iodex ointment is the best treatment; it should be applied every other day until the condition clears up. Surgery is seldom permanently successful.

Arthritis. This sometimes affects the joints of older dogs, causing pain and limping. Dogs suffering from it should be kept warm and dry; treatment with anti-inflammatory drugs is sometimes effective.

Hip dysplasia. Many of the larger breeds of dog are prone to this malformation of the hip joint, and the St Bernard is no exception. The reasons for its incidence are not fully understood, but hereditary factors are believed to play a part. In the normal hip joint, the acetabulum (socket) on the pelvis is a deep rounded hollow into which the head of the femur (ball) fits closely. In the dysplastic joint, the socket is shallow, and the femoral head is flattened instead of rounded. The ball is thus incompletely engaged in the socket, and when palpated the joint feels loose and slightly disjointed. The ligaments attached to the joint may be loose or torn, and the cartilage covering the socket and ball may become affected, causing pain during movement, with consequent abnormality of movement. Arthritic symptoms may ensue, as a result of friction in the ill-fitting joint.

Hip dysplasia is investigated by X-ray, and may vary from slight cases, where there is a poor fit between the ball and the socket, to very severe manifestations, where the socket is completely flattened and the head of the femur displaced entirely. Mild cases will usually improve as the muscles develop and grow to hold the joint in place. Many growing St Bernards exhibit looseness of gait and apparent stiffness in the hind legs, and many veterinary surgeons grow rich by alarming owners about the severity of very slight degrees of abnormality in the hip joint.

The British Veterinary Association and the Kennel Club now have a new Hip Scoring Scheme, which is a fresh attempt to tackle the problem. The aim is to X-ray and 'score' as many dogs in a breed as possible, so that average data for that particular breed can be calculated. When interpreting results, the lower the score, the less the degree of hip dysplasia. A total score of 4 or less, with not more than 3 on either hip, can be regarded as HD free, while a total score of 8, with not more than 6 on either hip, is regarded as a second grade 'pass'. The maximum possible score is 53 for each hip, giving a total of 106. The data, not the individual scores, are made available to Breed Societies, in the hope that they will encourage the use for breeding of dogs whose scores are below the breed average. In this way, and assuming the absence of non-hereditary factors, there should be progressive improvement in the hip scores of each generation of progeny. Until show judges, both specialists and all-rounders, penalise exhibits showing unsound hind movement, it will be difficult to make much progress in eliminating the disease completely; selectivity, breeding only from the soundest animals, is essential.

Research during the last decade has shown a correlation between the weight of the muscle-mass surrounding the hip joint, and the incidence of dysplasia. Greyhounds, which never exhibit dysplasia, have been found to have a higher pelvic muscle-mass in proportion to their total body weight than other breeds, and this applies even if the animals have not been trained for racing. Treatment to build up the muscle-mass with drugs has been tried with some success; vitamin E has long been known to assist muscular development. It has also been demonstrated that puppies which gain the most weight during the first few months of life are the most likely to have poor hip structure, while puppies which gain weight slowly and regularly are less at risk.

INFECTIOUS DISEASES

The greatest possible boon to the modern dog-breeder has been the development of vaccines against distemper, hard-pad and other infectious diseases. In the past it was common for whole kennels to be wiped out if one dog picked up an infection at a show. In addition to distemper and hard-pad, dogs can now be protected against *Leptospira canicola*, which attacks the kidneys, and *Leptospira icterohaemorrhagic*, an infection caught from rats, which causes a form of jaundice, and *contagious virus heptatitis* (Rubarth's disease) which attacks the liver.

It is most important that breeders selling young puppies should impress upon purchasers that their new pets must not be allowed to mix with other dogs, or visit public places, until immunised at eleven or twelve weeks.

EMERGENCIES

Heatstroke. This condition is associated with excessively hot weather and great exertion. It is commonly caused when thoughtless owners leave dogs shut in cars on which the sun beats down. Even with the windows open, the unfortunate dog may find himself imprisoned in what is virtually an oven, and may collapse and suffer convulsions. An affected dog must be immediately removed to a cool, shady place, and have his head, neck and chest doused with cold water. Ice packs, if available, are a great help, and the dog must be allowed to rest quietly for as long as possible.

Heart attacks. Undue exertion or excitement may cause a dog with any abnormal heart condition to fall over on its side, apparently in a 'faint'. The sufferer should be laid in an airy place, with his head lower than the rest of his body, to improve the circulation of blood to the brain. It may be necessary to apply artificial respiration if the breathing is impaired. If the attacks persist veterinary advice should be sought.

Epileptic fits. The distressing symptoms of fits need no description here. Any sufferer should be held down under a blanket to prevent injury during the convulsive movements. He should be examined by a vet as soon as possible.

Poisoning. If a dog is known to have swallowed a poisonous substance, such as weekiller or rat poison, one should try to make him sick by giving an emetic of strong salt solution or a lump of washing soda. He should be taken to the surgery without delay.

Stings. If possible the sting should be extracted (in the case of a wasp it will have been withdrawn by the insect itself). The area should be bathed with strong bicarbonate of soda solution, or, if inside the mouth, with spirit such as whisky. Stings in the throat are highly dangerous, and need prompt veterinary attention.

Burns and scalds. St Bernards investigating the pans on top of their owners' cooking stoves have often been known to upset the contents over themselves. It is wise to keep a tube of Acriflavine handy for use in this and any similar emergency. If the injury is severe, the dog should be treated for shock and kept warm and quiet. He should be encouraged to drink as much as possible. The hair should be clipped from the wound, which should be covered with a dressing soaked in bicarbonate of soda solution (1 oz per pint or 45 g/l). Every precaution must be taken to prevent the wounds from becoming septic. If the burn or scald is so deep that the hair roots are destroyed, the coat will not grow again.

Road accidents. Only a very negligent owner will allow his dog to wander on the road, and risk injury to himself and others in this way. If it does happen it is best to avoid moving the dog, and try to keep him warm until the vet arrives. If he must be moved he should be placed on an improvised stretcher with the injured part uppermost.

In accidents involving a St Bernard, the vehicle sometimes suffers more damage than the dog. A St Bernard running loose on the M1 Motorway near here (not one of ours) caused a three-car pile-up, and when the vet was called to attend to the dog he found it to be suffering only mild shock, although it had been hit by the leading car. We always say their skulls are thick!

OLD AGE

It is often said that St Bernards, like other big breeds, do not have a long life-span. This must depend greatly on how well the individual dog is cared for. If adequately fed and exercised, there is no reason why a normal Saint should not be active and healthy until the age of at least ten years and over, provided he is *not* allowed to become *too fat*. The record life-span is, I believe, sixteen, so, failing accident or organic disease, there is no reason why dogs of this breed should not become 'senior citizens'.

When an elderly St Bernard begins to 'slow up', he should be specially cosseted and allowed to live at his own speed; he will probably not be too anxious to get up in the mornings! He may be more comfortable on two small meals daily instead of one large one. He should have a warm, cosy bed, and if possible live in the house rather than in kennels.

If prompt veterinary assistance is sought when the various physical weaknesses of old age first begin to show themselves, life-span can often be comfortably prolonged. Rapid breathing and a cough sometimes indicate early heart trouble, which can be helped by various pills; excessive thirst may be a symptom of kidney disease, metritis, or even diabetes, and quick diagnosis of these ailments may keep them at bay for some time.

When the sad time comes and an old favourite ceases to find life a pleasure, he deserves the kindness of a painless death. Always ask the vet to come to the house, and stay with him while the painless injection is given. Never leave him at the surgery to face death alone in a strange place, among people he does not know. After all the pleasure he has given you, you owe him this last consideration.

16 St Bernard Breed Clubs

Since St Bernards were first introduced into this country during the nineteenth century, there have been a number of associations formed to promote the breeding of the correct type of Saint, and to encourage its exhibition.

The first such organisation, known as *The St Bernard Club*, was founded in 1882, and amassed a very valuable collection of trophies some of which are still in existence. Writing in the Club Year Book of 1913, L. C. R. Norris-Elye gives an interesting account of the earlier days of this Club, and of its first shows.

'The St Bernard Club entered on its great career in the year 1882 when some of the many enthusiasts of the breed came to the conclusion that the unity of a great Club would give them more power to help the breed than the individual efforts of isolated persons in different parts of the British Isles, enthusiastic though they might be. The Club was formed, a Committee appointed, with Mr J. C. Macdona as President, and the Rev. Arthur Carter as Secretary. The Duke of Wellington took the matter up also, and lent his beautiful Riding School at Knightsbridge for the first three Shows. The carelessness of workmen leaving nails about, and endangering the horses who used the Riding School after the dog benches were removed, led to the building being in future refused for the purpose, and the Club shows were held in different places and sometimes in connection with another great show.

'In 1882 the FIRST SHOW was judged by Mr Macdona, who showed, not for competition, the great Bayard, and his son Boniface; and among other celebrities shown there were Save Dunstan, Amy, Leonard, Alpenstock III, Barry, and others. Entries numbered 252. Afterwards came a period of troubled waters, to which it is now unnecessary to refer: de mortuis etc. But re-organisation became necessary, and was effected at a meeting, to attend which I had to come over from France. It may amuse some of you members to learn that one of the reasons given by my proposer for my election on the Committee, was that I was 'a fast bowler'.

'The SECOND SHOW, in 1883, again at Knightsbridge, was judged by the Rev. A. Carter and the late Mr S. W. Smith, and obtained 264 entries. The principal exhibits, in addition to many of the above mentioned, were Glacier, Cadwallader, Faust, Pilgrim (sire of Plinlimmon), Dignity and Sirius (Precipice was already dead as a yearling).

'The THIRD SHOW, in 1884, judged by Messrs. J. F. Smith and A. B. Bailey, produced 247 entries, and was remarkable for the appearance of the Rev. A. Carter's fortunate purchase Plinlimmon, and his beautiful bitch Thisbe; also among the winners were Valentine, Sultan III, Nero III, Duchess of Leeds, Hector II, and Lady Eva, in addition to those previously mentioned.

'The FOURTH SHOW, held at Southport, in June 1886, was judged by the Rev. A. Carter and Mr H. G. Sweet, and produced 170 entries. Many good new ones were here. Sir Charles, Lord Warwick, Lady Grace, Tempest Watchman, Bessie II (dam of Plinlimmon) etc.

'The SIXTH SHOW was held in the same year, December 1886, in the Albert Palace, Battersea. Judged by Mr J. F. Smith and Mr W. B. Megone, entries were 201. The new faces included Guide, Prince Battenberg, Kastelhorn, St Gothard, Sea King and others.

'The SEVENTH SHOW, in 1887, was held at Lillie Bridge, and was judged by Mr S. W. Smith, and Mr F. E. Elton. Entries 226. The new faces here were Angelow, Puritan, Refuge II, Reuben, Rustic, Carrichblacher General, Sans Peur, etc.

'The EIGHTH SHOW, in 1887, was held at Sheffield, and judged by Mr F. J. Smith and Mr L. Oppenheim. The entries were 217 in number, and the show was the first of our Club Shows at which the great SIR BEDIVERE, and the beautiful KEEPER and WATCH appeared. Also ALTON, Prince Regent, Dermot, Lord Bute, Peggotty, Abyss, Atlantic (wittily so called by Mr Sweet because he was not Pacific in his temper), Nun Nicer, Duke of Norfolk, Priest; a grand lot of new names.

'The NINTH SHOW, in 1889, was held at WINDSOR, at the same time as 'The Royal'. Unfortunately, the route to the Royal was changed at the last moment, so the crowd instead of passing the entrance to the St Bernard Club Show was diverted to another road, ruining our gate money, as well as injuring many tradesmen who had rented plots on the original route. The judges were the Rev. Arthur Carter and Mr G. W. Marsden, and the entries numbered 202. This was the first of the St Bernard Club Shows to be held under K. C. Rules. Those before this time were held under our own rules, but many of us had felt for some time that though we did not like in every respect the constitution of the Kennel Club, it was in the general interest that all shows should be held under the same rules, and subject in some degree to some Central Authority. The new names Princess Florence, Neophyte, Aristocrat, Oliver Twist,

Young Wellington, Lady Sneerwell, Vega (afterwards, I think, called Andromeda), and others.

'The TENTH SHOW, in 1890, was held at Olympia, judged by myself and Mr L. Oppenheim. Entries 230. The new faces were – so far as I can recollect – Proctor, Salvator Rosa (who had a great innings) Daddy's Donovan, the great Sir Hereward (the best eight months old puppy ever shown, but he did not grow later as much as could have been wished, perhaps because he was shown so young. His head was a perfect picture, and the most perfect St Bernard head I ever saw).

'The ELEVENTH SHOW, in 1891, was held at the Bingley Hall, Birmingham, and was judged by Mr Sweet and the Rev. A. Carter. Entries 182. There were some lovely new faces among the fresh aspirants. Fresh comers were Young Bute, Minstrel Boy (entered but absent), Geraint, Refugee, Waterbury (a wickedly-named son of Watch), Young Custos (a cross of the Keeper and Sir Hereward strains, and one of the loveliest-headed dogs I ever saw; destined to die by accident soon after this show), Lola IV, with a great career before her, Chiquita, etc. This show was remarkable as the first in which a bitch won the Trophy against the 100 Guineas Challenge Cup winning dog, my Alta Bella pulling it off against Keeper Angelo, Young Bute, and other celebrities. Since then the fair sex have been successful on more than one occasion.

'The TWELFTH SHOW was held in 1893 at Kingston, and was judged by Mr Gresham and myself. Entries 146. The principal new winners were Starboard, Binnacle, Mozart, Mountain Guard, Hitchin, Lady Mignon, Sans Reproche, and others.

From this period, if I am not mistaken, the Club shows were held in connection with other great shows, especially with the Kennel Club shows at the Crystal Palace and with the re-established show at Birmingham. On the resignation of Mr Cumming Macdona, I was elected President in his place, and when I resigned on coming to live so far from London, Mr J. F. Smith succeeded me; on his resignation Mr Marsden occupied the place, which he still holds with such advantage to the Club.

'In closing this very brief account of the Earlier Days of the St Bernard Club, and the dogs exhibited at its shows, I may perhaps be allowed to add two stories of Committees which have always amused me. One referred to a dog sold to America, when a member said: " I have always wondered why Blank sold Blank to America?" The late Mr Sweet, in his dry way, said: "Perhaps to improve the breed of St Bernards in *England*". It is unnecessary to remark that Mr Sweet was not an admirer of the dog in question. Another arose from the mistaken habit of quoting great puppy weights, which came into fashion after the glories of Plinlimmon had caused rather a craze for size. One very popular member used to be a great deal chaffed about his puppy weights, the animals being in his opinion "as lean as a rail", or "in just hard conditions", though others thought them too fat. A present leading member of the Club, business being over, suddenly startled the committee by saying; "Now, Mr President, let us see who can tell the biggest lie about our puppies' weights! What do you think, Blank, of a puppy only sixteen weeks old weighing X pounds? – naming some quite impossible weight. The heavy weight man turned round with anxiety on every feature: "No! Have you really had one that reached that, at that age?" Reply: "Well, no, I have not at present but I may have some day; you can never tell!" Many other good stories might be told of those happy days, but some would be at the expense of other people, so are best left unprinted.

'For myself, I must say that the kindness and courtesy I received, whether as Committee-man, Vice President, President, or Judge, have left a deep impression on me, and I trust similar treatment of its officials may always be characteristic of the Club'.

L. C. R. NORRIS-ELYE

It is sad to report that apparently the St Bernard Club failed to maintain the high standards that Mr Norris-Elye attributed to it, and began to lose support until it was wound up in 1920, when the English St Bernard Club came into existence.

The *National St Bernard Club* was founded in 1899, largely as a result of the efforts of Dr Inman. It arose from the Liverpool and Northern Counties St Bernard Club, begun by Messrs Foster and Bowley in 1893 to serve the interests of breeders living in the North of England. In its heyday, the National Club was a strong and well-supported organisation, with many valuable trophies, but by 1919 it had no Secretary, and appears to have been wound up shortly afterwards.

The *United St Bernard Club* was founded in 1928, at a meeting held at the Ladies Kennel Association Show on 3 May, 'in view of the then prevailing dissatisfaction with the conduct of St Bernard affairs, and to satisfy the demand for an efficient and helpful organisation, worthy of the breed.' Its first President was Mr R. A. Staines, and Mr E. Chasty was its first Secretary. It set up an advisory bureau of six experienced members, whose task it was to give help and advice to newcomers. Mr G. Walker of the Peldartor Kennels was Secretary from 1958 for seventeen years. After his retirement the club ceased to function, as a result of a dispute among its members, but it was re-established in 1980. It held its first Championship show at Rugby in 1985 with Mrs Gwen Broadley judging. Best in Show went to Mr and Mrs M. Wensley's Smooth Ch. Swindridge Mathew. The Club operates a Rescue Scheme for unwanted St Bernards, of which there are sadly a most unfortunate number. Richard Beaver is now the United Club's President.

The *St Bernard Club of Scotland* was founded in 1922, but ceased to function during the war years. It was revived in 1952, and now plays a prominent role in St Bernard affairs. In 1975 it held the first Championship Show confined to St Bernards ever to be organised in this country. The judge was Mrs Clare Bradley, who made Ch. Lindenhall Capability Brown, Best in Show, and Ch. Coatham Star Shine, Best Opposite Sex. The present secretary is Mrs D. Gunn of the Arisaig St Bernards.

Mr and Mrs M. Wensley's Smooth Ch. Swindridge Mathew. Best in Show at the United St Bernard Club's first Championship Show in 1985.

When the original St Bernard Club and the National St Bernard Club, ceased to function in 1921, the present *English St Bernard Club* was formed, and took over their assets and trophies. Mr J. Redwood of the Pearl Kennels was its first Secretary. He was succeeded during the 1930s Mrs J. F. Briggs, who bred the Beldene St Bernards at Queensbury near Leeds. Mr A. K. Gaunt became Secretary in 1947 and continued to run the English Club until 1974. In April of that year the Club held its first Open Show, which drew an entry of 74 dogs. The first English Club Championship Show, organised by the present secretary, Miss P. M. Muggleton, was held at Bingham, near Nottingham, in March 1979, and drew an entry of 314, made by 148 dogs. The judge, Mr M. Whitelaw, chose Ch. Burtonswood Black Tarquin as Best in Show, and Ch. Coatham Star Shine as Best Bitch. Two regional clubs for the benefit of St Bernard breeders in the Eastern and Southern Counties of England have been set up since 1984.

In all Breed clubs, there are periods when the interests of the individuals take precedence over the interests of the breeds the clubs are ostensibly supposed to serve, and St Bernard Clubs have sometimes in the past failed in this respect. If the Kennel Club would lay down standard and carefully formulated rules governing the election of all Club Officials and Club Judges, many of these unsatisfactory situations could be avoided. It is the responsibility of all St Bernard Club members, who have the interests of the breed at heart, to attend meetings, and play their part in ensuring that affairs are conducted in such a way that the successful breeding and exhibition of 'The King of Dogs' will be advanced.

Appendix 1: Champions 1947–1986

Year	Champion	Sex	Date of Birth	Sire	Dam	Breeder	Owner	Challenge Certificates
1947	Yewtree St Christopher	Dog	14.9.43	Yew Tree St Bruno	Yew Tree St Filumena	Mrs C. E. Walker	A. K. Gaunt	3
1948	St Christopher	Dog	31.5.44	Clearbrook St John	Modern Miss	E. W. Dovey	E. Chasty	5
	Caesario of Clairvaux	Dog	14.7.44	Freizland Lion	St Cecilia of Clairvaux	Miss E. Watts	Miss E. Watts	3
	Cornagarth Wendy of Flossmere	Bitch	8.9.42	Jupiter of Priorsleigh	Prudence of Priorsleigh	T. Lightfoot	A. K. Gaunt	6
	Clearbrook Sally	Bitch	13.9.44	Clearbrook St John	My Lady Jane	Miss L. A. Laidlaw	Miss I. L. Gross	4
	Mountains Gypsy Girl	Bitch	26.2.46	Copleydene Lucky Flight	Lady of the Mountains	Mr & Mrs E. Farragher	Mrs A. E. Irving	5
1949	Cornagarth Mountains Tiger	Dog	20.7.44	Copleydene Lucky Flight	Zena of the Mountains	Mr & Mrs E. Farragher	A. K. Gaunt	4
	Yew Tree St Errol of Priorsleigh	Dog	28.3.44	Yew Tree St Bruno	Yew Tree St Filumena	Mrs C. E. Walker	Mrs N. Cox	3
	Molino St Brittania	Bitch	6.3.45	Ch. Yew Tree St. Christopher	Yew Tree St Anne	Dr E. Heard	A. K. Gaunt	3
	Lady St Maidell	Bitch	10.1.46	Copleydene Lucky Flight	Alpine Lady	Miss J. Walkden	Miss J. Walkden	3
	Snowbound Traveller's Joy of St Olam	Dog	21.9.44	St Marcus	Lady of Trees	Mr Wilder	W. D. Joslin	3
1950	Snowbound Beau Cherie of St. Olam	Bitch	23.9.48	Snowbound Traveller's Joy of St-Olam	Snowbound Lassie	Mrs D. C. Wilder	W. D. Joslin	8
	Cornagarth Cornborrow St Ernesto	Dog	18.10.48	Ch. Yew Tree St Christopher	Ch. Lady St Maidell	Miss J. Walkden	A. K. Gaunt	3
	Cornagarth Bulldrummond of St Bury	Dog	2.10.46	St. Marcuson	Copleydene St Lionetta	W. F. Barazetti	A. K. Gaunt	3
	Thornebarton Bruno	Dog	23.9.46	Robin of Priorsleigh	Yew Tree St Gloria	Mrs C. E. Walker	Mrs G. M. Slazenger	3
	Mountains Glamour Girl	Bitch	16.4.45	Copleydene Lucky Flight	Zena of the Mountains	Mr & Mrs E Farragher	Mrs E. Graydon Bradley	7
1951	Moorgate Violet	Bitch	5.9.44	Beldene Barco	Moorgate May	W. Barton	A. J. Gaunt	3
	Boystown Cavalier	Dog	25.6.45	Robin of Priorsleigh	Yew Tree St Beatrice	Mrs N. Cox	Mrs E. Graydon Bradley	5
	St Dominic of Brenchley	Dog	7.8.47	St Jude of Brenchley	Abbess of Brenchley	J. B. Knock	Mrs R. L. Walker	3
	Cornagarth Culzean Nero	Dog	27.12.49	Ch. Yew Tree St Christopher	Beldene Josephine	Mrs R. M. Bryce	A. K. Gaunt	3
	Cornagarth Colonel	Dog	18.6.47	Ch. Yew Tree St Christopher	Cornagarth Sandra	A. K. Gaunt	W. A. Jeffery & H. Wilkinson	3
	St Olam Regent Prince	Dog	2.11.49	St Marcuson	Cynthia of St Olam	W. D. Joslin	W. D. Joslin	4
	Cornagarth Cornborrow St Oliver	Dog	18.10.48	Ch. Yew Tree St Christopher	Ch. Lady St Maidell	Miss J. Walkden	A. K. Gaunt	3
	Cornagarth Brenda	Bitch	13.7.47	Cornagarth Gulliver	Cornagarth Georgia	A. K. Gaunt	Mrs A. Rees	3
	Melody of Priorsleigh	Bitch	30.6.46	Robin of Priorsleigh	Yew Tree St Beatrice	Mrs N. Cox	Mrs N. Cox	3
	Cornagarth Betty	Bitch	13.7.47	Cornagarth Gulliver	Cornagarth Georgia	A. K. Gaunt	A. K. Gaunt	3

Year	Name	Sex	Date	Sire	Dam			No.
1952	Brenda of Peldartor	Bitch	16.7.49	Ch. St Dominic of Brenchley	Cornagarth Belinda	Mrs R. L. Walker	Mrs R. L. Walker	3
	Beldene Portia	Bitch	27.12.48	Daphnydene Bruno of Beldene	Daphnydene Annabella	Mrs J. F. Briggs	A. K. Gaunt	3
	Mairead Masterpiece	Dog	27.12.49	Ch. Yew Tree St Christopher	Beldene Josephine	Miss R. M. Bryce	Miss R. M. Bryce	5
	Cornagarth Marshall Von Zwing Uri	Dog	7.4.47	Hasso Von Zwing Uri	Christel Von Moosberg	C. Sigrist	A. K. Gaunt	4
1953	Cornagarth Guardsman	Dog	5.4.51	Ch. Cornagarth Marshall Von Zwing Uri	Ch. Cornagarth Cornborrow St Catherine	A. K. Gaunt	A. K. Gaunt	5
	Carol of Peldartor	Bitch	6.1.50	Beldene Mikado	Cornagarth Dawn	Mrs R. L. Walker	Mrs R. L. Walker	3
	Cornagarth Cornborrow St Catherine	Bitch	18.10.48	Ch. Yew Tree St Christopher	Ch. Lady St Maidell	Miss J. Walkden	A. K. Gaunt	3
	St Olam Sultan	Dog	15.8.51	Ch. St Olam Regent Prince	Zena of St Olam	W. D. Joslin	W. D. Joslin	4
	Colossus of Peldartor	Dog	6.1.50	Beldene Mikado	Cornagarth Dawn	Mrs R. L. Walker	Mrs R. L. Walker	3
	Cornagarth McNab	Dog	27.12.49	Ch. Yew Tree St Christopher	Beldene Josephine	Mrs M. Bryce	Mrs M. Whiteley	5
1954	Peldartor Anka Von der Ducke Schlense	Bitch	22.12.48	Conny Von der Eilshorst	Undine V. Hammoverland	Herr Otto Harder	Mrs R. L. Walker	3
	Terwin Caliph	Dog	8.5.49	Ch. Yew Tree St Christopher	Clovella of Priorsleigh	H. M. Bunting & N. M. Shorter	H. M. Bunting	3
	Margurita of Normadene	Bitch	7.8.51	Ch. Cornagarth Marshall V. Zwing Uri	Cornagarth Heatherbelle	Mrs M. Whiteley	Mrs M. Whiteley & Mr N. Davies	6
1955	Cornagarth Monberno Anthony	Dog	4.1.51	Beldene Ajax	Monberno Belle	Rev M. Brasil	A. K. Gaunt	3
	What a Girl	Bitch	24.4.52	The Ace of Mountsonia	St Winifred	Mrs L. Townley	Mrs L. Townley	3
	Mairead Indian Prince	Dog	27.12.49	Ch. Yew Tree St Christopher	Beldene Josephine	Miss R. M. Bryce	Miss R. M. Bryce	3
	Peldartor Lydia	Bitch	1.11.52	Ch. Colossus of Peldartor	Ch. Brenda of Peldartor	Mrs R. L. Walker	Mrs R. L. Walker	3
1956	Monberno Duke	Dog	4.1.51	Beldene Ajax	Monberno Belle	Rev M. Brasil	Mrs O. A. Lees	4
	Cornagarth Christopher	Dog	4.10.51	Ch. Cornagarth Colonel	Ch. Cornagarth Betty	A. K. Gaunt	A. K. Gaunt	3
	Brownie of St Bury	Bitch	4.10.51	Ch. Yew Tree St Christopher	Angelica of St Bury	W. Barazetti	W. Barazetti	3
	Snowbound Cynthia	Bitch	3.4.51	Snowbound Avalanche Lionheart	Joy of Snowbound Lassie	Mrs D. Wilder	Miss D. Wilder	3
	Peldartor Lucia	Bitch	1.11.52	Ch. Colossus of Peldartor	Ch. Brenda of Peldartor	Mrs R. L. Walker	Mrs R. L. Walker	3
	Cornagarth Limelight	Dog	10.4.53	Ch. Cornagarth Culzean Nero	Cornagarth My Own	J. Quigley	A. K. Gaunt	3
	Cornagarth Crysella	Bitch	4.10.51	Ch. Cornagarth Col.	Ch. Cornagarth Betty	A. K. Gaunt	A. K. Gaunt	3
	Peldart or Charnwood Bruno	Dog	15.1.52	Beldene Ajax	Monberno Belle	Rev M. Brasil	Mrs R. L. Walker	3
	St Olam Beauty	Bitch	15.9.53	St Olam Mischa	St Olam Reedcourt St Babette	W. D. Joslin	W. D. Joslin	3

Year	Champion	Sex	Date of Birth	Sire	Dam	Breeder	Owner	Challenge Certificates
	Peldartor Orrangit	Dog	4.1.54	Ch. Peldartor Charnwood Bruno	Ch. Carol of Peldartor	Mrs R. L. Walker	Mrs R. L. Walker	3
	Mairead Angus McNab	Dog	17.9.54	Ch. Mairead Masterpiece	Ch. Snowbound Cynthia	Miss R. M. Bryce	Miss R. M. Bryce	6
1957	Christcon St Anthony	Dog	21.5.54	Ch. Cornagarth Culzean Nero	Cornagarth Comet	Mrs C. Hutchings	Mrs C. Hutchings	12
	Peldartor Ranee	Bitch	13.6.55	Ch. Peldartor Charnwood Bruno	Ch. Peldartor Anka v.d. Schlense	Mrs R. L. Walker	Mrs R. L. Walker	5
	Cornagarth Durrowabbey St Teresa	Bitch	1.6.54	Ch. Cornagarth Cornborrow St Oliver	Ch. Cornagarth Thornebarton Jungfrau	Mrs G. Slazenger	A. K. Gaunt	3
	Cornagarth Thornebarton Jungfrau	Bitch	20.9.51	Ch. Cornagarth Marshall V. Zwing Uri	Daphnydene Maxine	Mrs G. Slazenger	A. K. Gaunt	3
	Cornagarth Durrowabbey St Maria	Bitch	1.6.54	Ch. Cornagarth Cornborrow St Oliver	Ch. Cornagarth Thornebarton Jungfrau	Mrs G. Slazenger	A. K. Gaunt	4
1958	Peldartor Rosseau	Dog	13.6.55	Ch. Peldartor Charnwood Bruno	Ch. Peldartor Anka v.d. Schlense	Mrs R. L. Walker	Mrs R. L. Walker	3
	Bernmont Felicity	Bitch	21.5.54	Cornagarth Recorder of Bernmont	Bernmont Abbess	Mrs E. Muggleton	J. Harpham	3
	Christcon St Arline	Bitch	21.5.54	Ch. Cornagarth Culzean Nero	Cornagarth Comet	Mrs C. Hutchings	Mrs C. Hutchings	3
	Cornagarth Harvest of Durrowabbey	Bitch	8.8.56	Castor Von Ringelli	Ch. Cornagarth Durrowabbey St Teresa	A. K. Gaunt	A. K. Gaunt	3
	Cornagarth Just Right	Dog	25.9.56	Ch. Cornagarth Limelight	Cornagarth Netta	Mrs A. A. Newton	A. K. Gaunt	3
	Cornagarth Falco	Dog	23.6.54	Ch. Cornagarth Guardsman	Ch. Cornagarth Crysella	A. K. Gaunt	A. K. Gaunt	3
1959	Cornagarth Brittainia of Durrowabbey	Bitch	31.5.57	Ch. Cornagarth Guardsman	Ch. Cornagarth Durrowabbey St Teresa	A. K. Gaunt	A. K. Gaunt	3
	Cornagarth Beverley of Durrowabbey	Bitch	31.5.57	Ch. Cornagarth Guardsman	Ch. Cornagarth Durrowabbey St Teresa	A. K. Gaunt	A. K. Gaunt	3
	Prima Donna of Burtonswood	Bitch	9.9.55	Ch. Peldartor Charnwood Bruno	Cornagarth Coronet	Miss M. Hindes	Miss M. Hindes	3
	Cornagarth Monbardon Sir Marcus	Dog	15.2.57	Cornagarth Durrowabbey St Patrick	Cornagarth Horsa	Mrs R. M. Clemerson	A. K. Gaunt	4
	Christcon St Iris	Bitch	18.2.57	Cornagarth Durrowabbey St Patrick	Cornagarth Comet	Mrs C. E. Hutchings	Mrs C. E. Hutchings	10
	Cornagarth Birthday Boy of Durrowabbey	Dog	11.3.58	Cornagarth Benedict of Solentvale	Ch. Cornagarth Durrowabbey St Teresa	A. K. Gaunt	A. K. Gaunt	3
1960	Cornagarth Defender of Durrowabbey	Dog	10.6.58	Ch. Cornagarth Falco	Ch. Cornagarth Durrowabbey St Maria	A. K. Gaunt	A. K. Gaunt	3
	Cornagarth Vanetta	Bitch	14.2.56	Ch. Cornagarth Christopher	Cornagarth Tosca	A. K. Gaunt	A. K. Gaunt	3
	Cornagarth Delilah of Durrowabbey	Bitch	10.6.58	Ch. Cornagarth Falco	Ch. Cornagarth Durrowabbey St Maria	A. K. Gaunt	A. K. Gaunt	3

Year	Name	Sex	Date					No.
	Cornagarth Monbardon Sir Jonathen	Dog	15.2.57	Cornagarth Durrowabbey St Patrick	Cornagarth Horsa	Mrs R Clemerson	Mrs C. Bradley	3
	Garry of Bryneithin	Dog	10.8.54	Bryneithin Masterpiece	Bryneithin Sandra of Normandene	Mrs S. Lawton	Dr U. Westell	4
	Cornagarth Pied Piper	Dog	3.4.57	Cornagarth Durrowabbey St Patrick	Cornagarth Crystal	Mr B. Cherry	Mr H. Allen	5
1961	Cornagarth Swiss Duchess	Bitch	21.3.56	Ch. Cornagarth Culzean Nero	Cornagarth Swiss Charmer	A. K. Gaunt	A. K. Gaunt	3
	Juno of Gresham	Bitch	18.9.58	Ch. Cornagarth Just Right	Cornagarth Veronica	Mrs B. Dew	Mrs G. M. Allen	5
	Cornagarth Burtonswood Easter Hero	Dog	31.3.58	Ch. Cornagarth Just Right	Ch. Prima Donna of Burtonswood	Miss M. Hindes	A. K. Gaunt	3
	Christcon Jeremy	Dog	24.2.57	Christcon St Barco	St Colliers Genevieve	Mrs D. Harrison	Mrs C. E. Hutchings	4
1962	Cornagarth Keep On	Dog	7.11.59	Ch. Cornagarth Defender of Durrowabbey	Ch. Prima Donna of Burtonswood	Miss M. Hindes	A. K. Gaunt	3
	Cornagarth Master of Durrowabbey	Dog	10.5.59	Ch. Peldartor Rosseau	Cornagarth Durrowabbey St Maria	A. K. Gaunt	A. K. Gaunt	3
	Peldartor Cornagarth Nicholas	Dog	11.3.58	Cornagarth Benedict of Solentvale	Cornagarth Durrowabbey St Teresa	A. K. Gaunt	Mrs R. L. Walker	3
	Burtonswood Katrina	Bitch	7.11.59	Ch. Cornagarth Defender of Durrowabbey	Ch. Prima Donna of Burtonswood	Miss M. Hindes	Miss M. Hindes	3
	Cornagarth Excellence	Dog	15.1.61	Ch. Cornagarth Defender of Durrowabbey	Cornagarth Robina	A. K. Gaunt	A. K. Gaunt	3
	Cornagarth Moira	Bitch	19.2.60	Ch. Cornagarth Monbardon Sir Marcus	Peldartor Wydello	Mrs A. N. Groves	A. K. Gaunt	4
1963	Cornagarth Marina	Bitch	19.2.60	Ch. Cornagarth Monbardon Sir Marcus	Peldartor Wydello	Mrs A. N. Groves	A. K. Gaunt	3
	Burtonswood Christcon St Olga	Bitch	26.8.58	Ch. Christcon St Jeremy	Christcon St Diana	Mrs C. Hutchings	Miss M. Hindes	4
	Cornagarth Sensation	Dog	22.4.59	Ch. Cornagarth Monbardon Sir Marcus	Cornagarth Berna	H. Tideswell	A. K. Gaunt	3
	Peldartor Xcellence	Dog	20.9.58	Peldartor Jacques	Peldartor Ritchell	Mrs R. L. Walker	Mrs R. L. Walker	4
1964	Fernebrandon Agrippa	Dog	28.6.61	Ch. Christcon St Jeremy	Fernebrandon Brita Von Salmegg	Mrs Dixon	Dr U. Westell	3
	Cornagarth Romaine of Durrowabbey	Bitch	29.10.61	Ch. Cornagarth Keep On	Ch. Cornagarth Delilah of Durrowabbey	A. K. Gaunt	A. K. Gaunt	3
	Cornagarth Democratic	Dog	10.6.58	Ch. Cornagarth Falco	Ch. Cornagarth Durrowabbey St Maria	A. K. Gaunt	A. K. Gaunt	3
	Cornagarth Minty of Maurbry	Bitch	10.9.61	Ch. Cornagarth Monbardon Sir Marcus	Burtonswood Easter Sue	Miss M. Hindes	Mrs M. Chapman	4

Year	Champion	Sex	Date of Birth	Sire	Dam	Breeder	Owner	Challenge Certificates
	Cornagarth for Tops	Dog	4.2.62	Ch. Cornagarth Monbardon Sir Marcus	Cornagarth Keep Me	A. K. Gaunt	A. K. Gaunt	5
	St Damian of Dale End	Dog	1.1.59	Ch. Cornagarth Just Right	St Elizabeth of Dale End	Mr & Mrs F. Read Pearson	Mr & Mrs F. Read Pearson	3
	Cornagarth to Treasure of Brondeg	Bitch	4.2.62	Ch. Cornagarth Monbardon Sir Marcus	Cornagarth Keep Me	A. K. Gaunt	A. K. Gaunt	4
	Peldartor Cornagarth Maracas	Dog	19.2.60	Ch. Cornagarth Monbardon Sir Marcus	Peldartor Wydello	Mrs A. N. Groves	Mrs R. L. Walker	3
1965	Fernebrandon Achilles	Dog	8.6.61	Ch. Christcon St Jeremy	Fernebrandon Britta Von Salmegg	Mrs Dixon	Dr J. Holmes	3
	Helga of Gresham	Bitch	15.10.58	Ch. Cornagarth Monbardon Sir Marcus	Gilda of Gresham	Mrs Dew	Mrs Dew	3
	Cornagarth Adam	Dog	30.5.62	Ch. Cornagarth Burtonswood Easter Hero	Christcon St Nadia	A. K. Gaunt	A. K. Gaunt	3
	Peldartor Ireton	Dog	20.4.61	Ch. Peldartor Cornagarth Nicholas	Ch. Peldartor Ranee	Mrs R. L. Walker	Mrs R. L. Walker	3
	Peldartor Julich	Bitch	14.11.61	Ch. Peldartor Cornagarth Nicholas	Ch. Peldartor Ranee	Mrs R. L. Walker	Mrs R. L. Walker	3
	Cornagarth Koon	Dog	30.12.62	Ch. Cornagarth Keep On	Cornagarth Debutant	Mrs M. Hall	A. K. Gaunt	3
	Cornagarth Cortina	Bitch	3.3.63	Ch. Cornagarth Keep On	Ch. Cornagarth Delilah of Durrowabbey	A. K. Gaunt	Dr & Miss Leonard	3
	Snowranger Arcadian	Dog	31.10.62	Ch. Cornagarth Keep On	Snowranger Lucky Charm	Mrs C. Bradley & Mr P. Hill	B. Driver	3
	Cornagarth Truthful	Bitch	7.3.63	Ch. Cornagarth Master of Durrowabbey	Ch. Cornagarth Moira	A. K. Gaunt	A. K. Gaunt	3
1966	Cornagarth Robin of Durrowabbey	Dog	29.10.61	Ch. Cornagarth Keep On	Ch. Cornagarth Delilah of Durrowabbey	A. K. Gaunt	A. K. Gaunt	3
	Cornagarth Wanda	Bitch	5.1.63	Cornagarth Memory of Durrowabbey	Cornagarth Elsa	A. K. Gaunt	A. K. Gaunt	3
	Peldartor Ruebens	Dog	30.12.63	Ch. Peldartor Xcellence	Ch. Peldartor Julich	Mrs R. L. Walker	Mrs R. L. Walker	3
	Cornagarth True Love	Bitch	7.3.63	Ch. Cornagarth Master of Durrowabbey	Ch. Cornagarth Moira	A. K. Gaunt	Miss M. Hindes	3
	Broxhead Cornagarth Annabelle	Bitch	17.8.61	Ch. Cornagarth Birthday Boy of Durrowabbey	Ch. Cornagarth Moira	A. K. Gaunt	Miss M. Hindes	3
	Cornagarth Demon	Dog	13.1.64	Ch. Cornagarth Democratic	Broxhead Cornagarth Sun Tan	Miss M. Hindes	A. K. Gaunt	3
	Panbride Lady Freda	Bitch	24.8.62	Ch. Christcon St Jeremy	Claypottis Lady Aurora	Miss J. Fyffe	Miss J. Fyffe	3
1967	Snowranger Chloris	Bitch	22.12.63	Snowranger Tello Von Saulient	Snowranger Saucy Sue	Mrs C. Bradley	Mrs C. Bradley & Mr P. Hill	3
	Kelvaston Sir Christopher	Dog	24.12.64	Ch. Cornagarth Sensation	Burtonswood Veronique	Dr & Miss Leonard	Dr & Miss Leonard	3
	Cornagarth Burtonswood Princess	Bitch	11.12.64	Ch. Cornagarth For Tops	Ch. Cornagarth True Love	Miss M. Hindes	A. K. Gaunt	3

Year	Name	Sex	Date	Sire	Dam	Breeder	Owner	No.
	Cornagarth To Be	Dog	4.2.62	Ch. Cornagarth Monbardon Sir Marcus	Cornagarth Keep Me	A. K. Gaunt	Lt Col Sir T. Cook	4
	Burtonswood Brown Velvet	Bitch	6.7.65	Ch. Cornagarth For Tops	Burtonswood Easter Sue	Miss M. Hindes	Miss M. Hindes	3
	Cornagarth Cordo	Dog	27.11.65	Ch. Cornagarth For Tops	Cornagarth Suzette	Dr Chesterfield	A. K. Gaunt	3
	Peldartor Abbott	Dog	6.6.65	Ch. Peldartor Xcellence	Peldartor Accra	Mrs R. L. Walker	Mrs R. L. Walker	3
	Bernmont Yana	Bitch	2.2.63	Ch. Christcon St Jeremy	Cornagarth Sophia	Mrs I. Oliver	Mrs & Miss Muggleton	3
1968	Cornagarth Stroller	Dog	27.10.66	Ch. Cornagarth Adam	Ch. Cornagarth Burtonswood Princess	A. K. Gaunt	A. K. Gaunt	4
	Cornagarth Mickado	Dog	16.12.63	Ch. Cornagarth Birthday Boy of Durrowabbey	Cornagarth Elsa	A. K. Gaunt	A. K. Gaunt	3
	Bernmont Warlord	Dog	10.11.64	Bernmont Snowranger Statesman	Bernmont Carol	Mrs & Miss Muggleton	Mrs & Miss Muggleton	8
	Burtonswood Cornagarth Molly	Bitch	20.6.66	Ch. Cornagarth For Tops	Cornagarth Melanie	A. K. Gaunt	Miss M. Hindes	3
	Cornagarth Burtonswood Bonanza	Dog	26.7.66	Ch. Cornagarth Keep On	Burtonswood Bitter Sweet	Miss M. Hindes	A. K. Gaunt	3
1969	Sennowe Riga	Bitch	24.11.64	Ch. Cornagarth To Be	Cornagarth Katrina	Lt Col Sir T. Cook	Lt Col Sir T. Cook	3
	Burtonswood Bright Star	Bitch	11.6.67	Ch. Cornagarth Adam	Burtonswood Bitter Sweet	Miss M. Hindes	Miss M. Hindes	6
	Cornagarth Carlos	Dog	8.9.67	Ch. Cornagarth Cordo	Cornagarth Carol	A. K. Gaunt	A. K. Gaunt	3
	Burtonswood Beloved	Bitch	13.5.68	Ch. Cornagarth Cordo	Burtonswood Bitter Sweet	Miss M. Hindes	Miss M. Hindes	5
	Bernmont Victoria	Bitch	1.10.64	Bernmont Christcon St Rajah	Bernmont Teresa	Mrs & Miss Muggleton	Mrs & Miss Muggleton	3
1970	Snowranger Bas Von der Vrouwenpolder	Dog	26.5.66	Hektor Von Liebiwil	Helga V. Hutwil	Mr A. Schrama	Mrs C. Bradley & Mr P. Hill	3
	Cornagarth Kelvaston Bo-Peep	Bitch	31.7.65	Ch. Cornagarth For Tops	Burtonswood Veronique	Dr & Miss Leonard	A. K. Gaunt	3
	Cornagarth He's Grand	Dog	18.6.68	Ch. Cornagarth Robin of Durrowabbey	Cornagarth Burtonswood Princess	A. K. Gaunt	A. K. Gaunt	3
	Burtonswood Black Diamond	Dog	11.1.69	Ch. Cornagarth Stroller	Burtonswood Be Wonderful	Miss M. Hindes	Miss M. Hindes	6
1971	Burtonswood Big Time	Bitch	6.2.68	Cornagarth Luck	Ch. Cornagarth True Love	Miss M. Hindes	M. J. Braysher	3
	Peldartor Zigismund	Dog	30.11.65	Ch. Peldartor Xcellence	Ch. Peldartor Julich	Mrs R. L. Walker	Mrs R. L. Walker	3
	Cornagarth Marquisite	Bitch	14.8.67	Ch. Cornagarth Koon	Cornagarth Cordette	A. K. Gaunt	Mrs M. Gwilliam	3
	Burtonswood Black Perle	Bitch	11.1.69	Ch. Cornagarth Stroller	Burtonswood Be Wonderful	Miss M. Hindes	Miss M. Hindes	3
	Cornagarth Shanta	Bitch	27.10.66	Ch. Cornagarth Adam	Ch. Cornagarth Burtonswood Princess	A. K. Gaunt	A. K. Gaunt	4

Year	Champion	Sex	Date of Birth	Sire	Dam	Breeder	Owner	Challenge Certificates
	Cornagarth Mirabelle	Bitch	4.8.67	Ch. Cornagarth Koon	Cornagarth Cordette	A. K. Gaunt	M. J. Braysher	3
	Cornagarth Luke	Dog	13.12.65	Ch. Cornagarth For Tops	Ch. Cornagarth Romaine of Durrowabbey	A. K. Gaunt	Mr J. & Miss P. Hill	3
	Ghyllendale Aristocrat	Bitch	16.11.69	Cornagarth Luck	Ghyllendale Cornagarth Juliana	Mr & Mrs B. Everall	Mr & Mrs B. Everall	3
1972	Burtonswood Be Bright	Bitch	15.6.70	Ch. Cornagarth Stroller	Ch. Burtonswood Beloved	Miss M. Hindes	Miss M. Hindes	4
	Cornagarth Fleur	Bitch	7.1.69	Ch. Cornagarth Stroller	Cornagarth Cordette	A. K. Gaunt	A. K. Gaunt	3
	Daphnydene Karro Von Birkenkopf	Dog	21.4.69	Alex Von Pava	Gundi Von Birkenkopf	O. Ulrich	Mrs D. Ackybourne	3
	Lindenhall High Commissioner	Dog	11.4.71	Cornagarth Kuno Von Birkenkopf	Cornagarth Adelaide	Mrs & Mrs R. J. Beaver	Mr & Mrs R. J. Beaver	15
	Burtonswood Bethney	Bitch	12.6.69	Ch. Cornagarth Stroller	Ch. Burtonswood Cornagarth Molly	Miss M. Hindes	Miss M. Hindes	3
	Bernmont Gilda	Bitch	8.8.69	Bernmont Iceberg	Cornagarth Michaela	Mrs M. Harris	Mrs & Miss Muggleston	4
	Burtonswood Be Mine	Bitch	15.6.70	Ch. Cornagarth Stroller	Ch. Burtonswood Beloved	Miss M. Hindes	Miss M. Hindes	3
	Cornagarth Burtonswood Be Great	Dog	15.6.70	Ch. Cornagarth Stroller	Ch. Burtonswood Beloved	Miss M. Hindes	A. K. Gaunt	3
1973	Burtonswood Bossy Boots	Dog	10.7.71	Cornagarth Kuno Von Birkenkopf	Ch. Burtonswood Beloved	Miss M. Hindes	Miss M. Hindes	13
	Cornagarth Heiki of Pittforth	Bitch	20.3.71	Cornagarth Kuno V. Birkenkopf	Cornagarth Burtonswood Becoming	A. K. Gaunt	Mr & Mrs M. Whitelaw	10
	Burtonswood Black Tarquin	Dog	16.12.70	Cornagarth Kuno V. Birkenkopf	Ch. Burtonswood Black Perle	Miss M. Hindes	A. K. Gaunt & Miss M. Hindes	13
	Bernmont Griselda	Bitch	8.8.69	Bernmont Iceberg	Cornagarth Michaela	Mrs M. Harris	Mrs & Miss Muggleston	3
	Panbride Sir Warran of Pittforth	Dog	4.8.68	Westernisles Fernebrandon Brutus	Panbride Lady Magnolia	Miss Milne	Mr & Mrs M. Whitelaw	3
	Burtonswood Bossy Bess	Bitch	10.7.71	Cornagarth Kuno V. Birkenkopf	Ch. Burtonswood Beloved	Miss M. Hindes	Miss M. Hindes	4
1974	Lindenhall Highlight	Bitch	11.4.71	Cornagarth Kuno V. Birkenkopf	Cornagarth Adelaide	Mr & Mrs R. J. Beaver	Mr & Mrs R. J. Beaver	5
	Burtonswood Be Able	Bitch	15.6.70	Ch. Cornagarth Stroller	Ch. Burtonswood Beloved	Miss M. Hindes	Mr & Mrs B. Loftus	4
	Pittforth Angus	Dog	21.1.73	Ch. Cornagarth Burtonswood Be Great	Ch. Cornagarth Heiki of Pittforth	Mr & Mrs M. Whitelaw	Mr & Mrs M. Whitelaw	4
	Snowranger Cascade	Dog	6.1.71	Snowranger Cornagarth Lucky	Snowranger Dresden	Mrs C. Bradley & Mr P. Hill	Miss J.McMurray	7
1975	Lindenhall High & Mighty	Bitch	11.4.71	Cornagarth Kuno V. Birkenkopf	Cornagarth Adelaide	Mr & Mrs R. J. Beaver	Mr & Mrs R. J. Beaver	4
	Lindenhall High Hopes	Bitch	8.6.70	Ch. Cornagarth Carlos	Anna Lisa of Thalberg	Mr & Mrs R. J. Beaver	Mr & Mrs R. J. Beaver	3
	Lindenhall High Commander	Dog	11.4.71	Cornagarth Kuno V. Birkenkopf	Cornagarth Adelaide	Mr & Mrs R. J. Beaver	Mr & Mrs R. J. Beaver	3
	Lindenhall Calamity Jane	Bitch	3.11.73	Ghyllendale Harvester	Ch. Lindenhall High & Mighty	Mr & Mrs R. J. Beaver	Mrs E. Ridley	11

Year	Name	Sex	DOB	Sire	Dam			No.
	Lindenhall Capability Brown	Dog	3.11.73	Ghyllendale Harvester	Ch. Lindenhall High & Mighty	Mr & Mrs R. J. Beaver	Mr & Mrs R. J. Beaver	7
	Cornagarth Cara	Bitch	27.8.72	Cornagarth Kuno V. Birkenkopf	Cornagarth Phoebe	A. K. Gaunt	Mrs G. Topping	3
1976	Burtonswood Black Lace	Bitch	2.8.73	Ch. Burtonswood Bossy Boots	Ch. Burtonswood Black Perle	Miss M. Hindes	Miss M. Hindes	3
	Burtonswood Be True	Dog	28.7.74	Ch. Burtonswood Bossy Boots	Cornagarth Chiquita	Miss M. Hindes	Mrs M. K. Humphrey	10
	Whaplode Desdemona	Bitch	9.9.73	Cornagarth Kuno V. Birkenkopf	Cornagarth Alma	Mr & Mrs J. Harpham	Mr & Mrs J. Harpham	5
	Whaplode Eros of Bernmont	Dog	16.2.74	Cornagarth Askan	Cornagarth Anna	Mr & Mrs J. Harpham	Mrs & Miss Muggleton	4
	Lindenhall High Ball	Dog	6.9.72	Ch. Lindenhall High Commissioner	Lindenhall Sweet Charity	Mr & Mrs R. J. Beaver	Mr & Mrs R. J. Beaver	3
1977	Coatham Star Shine	Bitch	13.11.73	Ch. Burtonswood Black Tarquin	Northern Star of Coatham	Mr & Mrs G. Gwilliam	Mr & Mrs G. Gwilliam	10
	Alpentire Paters Princess	Bitch	16.6.74	Ch. Cornagarth Burtonswood Be Great	Alpentire Snowranger Forest Charm	Mrs J. McMurray	Mrs J. McMurray	8
	Benem Lady Guinevere	Bitch	9.10.74	Lucky Strike of Cornagarth	My Lady Emma	Mr & Mrs R. Miller	Mr & Mrs M. Wensley	5
	Whaplode King	Dog	25.10.75	Whaplode Emporer	Burtonswood Black Jewel	Mr & Mrs J. Harpham	Mr & Mrs J. Harpham	3
	Lindenhall High Admiral	Dog	11.4.71	Cornagarth Kuno V. Birkenkopf	Cornagarth Adelaide	Mr & Mrs R. J. Beaver	Mrs D. Campbell	3
	Gerunda Buster	Dog	13.8.75	Prad King of Gerunda	Snowranger Lindsey	Messrs & Mrs James	Messrs & Mrs James	3
1978	Cornagarth Dominant Dominic of Bernmont	Dog	21.10.74	Ch. Burtonswood Black Tarquin	Braypass Audrey	A. K. Gaunt	Mrs & Miss Muggleton	4
	Lindenhall Fast & Furious	Bitch	3.4.74	Ch. Lindenhall High Commissioner	Ch. Lindenhall High Hopes	Mr & Mrs R. J. Beaver	Mr & Mrs R. J. Beaver	3
	Burtonswood Be Fine	Bitch	28.7.74	Ch. Burtonswood Bossy Boots	Cornagarth Chiquita	Miss M. Hindes	Mrs G. Topping	6
	Burtonswood Be Fire	Dog	28.7.74	Ch. Burtonswood Bossy Boots	Cornagarth Chiquita	Miss M. Hindes	Mrs J. Burr	3
	Pittforth Calum	Dog	6.12.75	Ch. Panbride Sir Warren of Pittforth	Ch. Cornagarth Heiki of Pittforth	Mr & Mrs M. Whitelaw	Mr & Mrs M. Whitelaw	3
1978	Whaplode Ivanhoe	Dog	27.3.75	Whaplode Emporer	Ch. Whaplode Desdemona	Mr & Mrs J. Harpham	Mr & Mrs J. Harpham	4
	Coatham Commissioner's Aide	Dog	23.3.75	Ch. Lindenhall High Commissioner	Northern Star of Coatham	Mr & Mrs G. Gwilliam	Mrs H. Taylor	3
	Braypass Sportsman	Dog	28.9.76	Ch. Burtonswood Bossy Boots	Braypass Butchers Girl	M. J. Braysher	M. J. Braysher	5
	Burtonswood Barensa	Bitch	4.1.74	Cornagarth Tough Nut	Ch. Burtonswood Bossy Bess	Miss M. Hindes	S. Oates	4
	Grand Duke of Lindenhall	Dog	26.3.76	Ch. Lindenhall Capability Brown	Hardacre Wotagem	Mrs A. Stepto	R. J. Beaver & Miss W. Machin	3

Year	Champion	Sex	Date of Birth	Sire	Dam	Breeder	Owner	Challenge Certificates
1979	Whaplode Margaret	Bitch	28.5.76	Ch. Whaplode Ivanhoe	Whaplode Amy	Mr and Mrs Harpham	as breeder	3
	Topvalley Wogans Winner	Dog	4.1.78	Ch. Burtonswood Bossy Boots	Lena of Cornagarth	Mrs G. Topping	as breeder	19
	Pittforth Catriona	Bitch	6.1.75	Ch. Panbride Sir Warran of Pittforth	Ch. Cornagarth Heiki of Pittforth	Mr and Mrs M. Whitelaw	as breeder	4
	Sandcroft Saroscha	Bitch	7.6.76	Ch. Burtonswood Black Tarquin	Burtonswood Benera	A. J. Osman	as breeder	6
	Lindenhall Sarah Siddons	Bitch	4.9.75	Ch. Lindenhall Capability Brown	Ch. Lindenhall Fast & Furious	Mr and Mrs R. Beaver	as breeder	5
	Topvalley Chardas	Dog	1.7.77	Ch. Burtonswood Bossy Boots	Burtonswood Black Secret	Mrs Topping	E. N. Davies	3
1980	Fairydales Demon King	Dog	30.7.76	Burtonswood Be Fire	Wildmere Natalia	Mrs J. Burr	E. J. Atkins	3
	Roddinghead Agent Kris of Knockespoch	Bitch	4.1.79	Alpentire Commission Agent	Roddinghead Prudence	A. Stevens	Mrs S. Roberts	10
	Swindridge Catherine	Bitch	10.3.77	King V. St Klara Kloster	Swindridge Madam Annaliese	Mr and Mrs M. Wensley	as breeders	4
	Burtonswood Be Friendly	Dog	27.4.77	Ch. Burtonswood Bossy Boots	Burtonswood Be Lovely	Miss M. Hindes	Mr and Mrs Scrivens	5
	Swindridge Madam Danielle	Bitch	9.8.77	Ch. Burtonswood Bossy Boots	Swindridge Madam Acacia	Mr and Mrs M Wensley	as breeder	3
	Whaplode Unique	Dog	2.6.78	Ch. Whaplode Ivanhoe	Whaplode Juliette	Mr and Mrs J. Harpham	as breeder	22
	Bernmont Nola	Bitch	1.4.76	Ch. Whaplode Eros of Bernmont	Benem Lady Constance of Bernmont	Mr and Miss Muggleton	as breeder	3
1981	Topvalley Joanne	Bitch	2.10.79	Topvalley Just Jamie	Topvalley Anna	Mrs G. Topping	as breeder	7
	Alpentire on Commission	Dog	8.2.77	Ch. Lindenhall High Commissioner	Alpentire Paters Promise	Mrs J. McMurray	G. Gwilliam	3
	Burtonswood Black Duke	Dog	13.3.76	Ch. Burtonswood Bossy Boots	Burtonswood Black Brocade	Miss M. Hindes	Mrs S. Boulden	3
	Maurbry Mini Sota of Bernmont	Bitch	30.3.77	Heidan Easter Greetings	Benem Lady Be Good	Mrs M. Chapman	Mrs & Miss Muggleton	4
	Swindridge Sir Dorian	Dog	9.8.77	Ch. Burtonswood Bossy Boots	Swindridge Madam Acacia	Mr and Mrs M. Wensley	as breeders	5
	Bernmont Aristocrat	Dog	29.9.78	Ch. Cornagarth Dominant Dominic of Bernmont	Bernmont Odessa	Mrs & Miss Muggleton	as breeders	3
	Be Elect of Burtonswood	Bitch	18.8.77	Ch. Burtonswood Bossy Boots	Braypass Olga	M. J. Braysher	Mr and Mrs Gwilliam	4
	Benem Sir Galahad	Dog	9.10.74	Lucky Strike of Cornagarth	My Lady Emma	Mrs R. Miller	Mrs J. Evans	8
	Be Glad of Burtonswood	Dog	24.8.77	Ch. Burtonswood Bossy Boots	Burtonswood Balrina	Mrs and Miss Cockings	E. G. Lloyd	4
	Topvalley Anna	Bitch	16.1.76	Ch. Burtonswood Bossy Boots	Toppos Delight	Mrs G. Topping	as breeder	3

Year	Name	Sex	Date	Sire	Dam	Owner		No.
1982	Burtonswood Be Mighty	Dog	29.8.79	Tweedle Dee of Burtonswood	Topvalley Carasel of Burtonswood	Miss M. Hindes	as breeder	4
	Braypass Boomerang	Bitch	26.8.79	Ch. Topvalley Wogans Winner	Braypass Special	M. J. Braysher	as breeder	3
	Bernmont Alexandra	Bitch	29.9.78	Ch. Cornagarth Dominant Dominic of Bernmont	Bernmont Odessa	Mr and Miss Muggleton	as breeder	3
	Irrissa of Bernmont	Bitch	12.1.80	Whaplode Julian of Bernmont	Pittforth Dallas	Mr and Mrs Whitelaw	Mrs and Miss Muggleton	3
	Swindridge Ferdinand	Dog	2.1.78	Ch. Swindridge Sir Dorian	Swindridge Catherine	Mr and Mrs Wensley	as breeders	4
	Pittforth Fleur	Bitch	15.1.80	Whaplode Julian of Bernmont	Pittforth Cassandra	Mr and Mrs M. Whitelaw	as breeders	4
	Morning Star of Hartleapwell	Bitch	7.2.80	Ch. Benem Sir Galahad	Icelandic Maiden of Hartleapwell	Mrs J. McMurray	Mrs J. Evans	4
	Ravensbank Hardtime	Bitch	7.12.77	Ch. Whaplode Ivanhoe	Whaplode Lucille	Mrs P. Stammers	as breeder	5
	Maubry Modelman	Dog	18.2.80	Ch. Topvalley Wogans Winner	Benem Lady Be Good	Mrs. M. Chapman	as breeder	3
1983	Lucky Charm of Whaplode	Bitch	10.4.81	Ch. Whaplode Unique	Ch. Roddinghead Agent Kris of Knockespoch	Mr and Mrs J. Harpham	as breeders	18
	Lady Prudence of Middlepark	Bitch	5.11.77	Ch. Benem Sir Galahad	Middlepark Harriet	Walker	Mrs S. Boulden	4
	Burtonswood Be Favourite	Dog	27.4.77	Ch. Burtonswood Bossy Boots	Burtonswood Be Lovely	Miss M. Hindes	as breeder	3
	Whaplode My Lord	Dog	25.4.81	Ch. Whaplode Ivanhoe	Whaplode Julliette	Mr and Mrs J. Harpham	as breeder	17
	Bernmont Charlotte	Bitch	21.6.79	Whaplode Julian of Bernmont	Bernmont Rhona	Mrs and Miss Muggleton	as breeders	4
	Swindridge Madam Hazel	Bitch	6.5.80	Swindridge Sir Edward	Swindridge Madam Acacia	Mr and Mrs M. Wensley	as breeders	3
	Bavush drina	Bitch	2.5.79	Whaplode Tobias	Fairydales Folly	Mrs T. Ridings	as breeders	5
1984	Laird O'Glayva of Treeburn	Dog	23.9.79	Alpentire Commission Agent	Icelandic Maiden of Hartleapwell	Miss C. Hennan	Mr and Mrs R. Gardner	5
	Knockespoch Berenice	Bitch	10.4.81	Ch. Whaplode Unique	Roddinghead Agent Kris of Knockespoch	Mrs S. Roberts	as breeder	5
	Maubry Message	Dog	4.10.80	Ch. Whaplode Unique	Benem Lady Be Good	Mrs M. Chapman	as breeder	3
	Mountain Hunter of Vallefrey	Dog	13.12.81	Ch. Whaplode Unique	Snowranbler of Adelja	Miss J. Peters	Mr and Mrs G. Craven	7
	Topvalley Karl	Dog	10.9.80	Ch. Topvalley Wogans Winner	Topvalley Carrin Withasea	Mrs G. Topping	as breeder	11
	Swindridge Madalene	B	1.4.82	Ch. Swindridge Ferdinand	Swindridge Geraldine	Mr and Mrs M. Wensley	as breeders	3
	Schnozzer Huggy Bear	Dog	23.7.83	Topvalley J.R.	Olympic Princess	Mr and Mrs P. Girling	as breeders	10
	Braypass Marina	Bitch	20.5.81	Ch. Cornagarth Dominant Dominic of Bernmont	Braypass Special	M. J. Braysher	as breeder	3
	Bernadino Maxi	Bitch	21.10.83	Ch. Topvalley Wogans Winner	Ravensbank Katy Cube of Bernadino	Mr and Mrs Lux	as breeders	9

Year	Champion	Sex	Date of Birth	Sire	Dam	Breeder	Owner	Challenge Certificates
1985	Merridale Bouncer	Dog	8.6.81	Topvalley Heidis Boy	Bavush Daydreamer	Clarke	Miss E. Cooper	6
	Swindridge Laura	Bitch	6.5.81	Ch. Swindridge Ferdinand	Swindridge Geraldine	Mr and Mrs M. Wensley	Mr and Mrs P. Girling	5
	Knockespoch Highline	Bitch	2.5.83	Knockespoch Boy	Fastacre Royale Empress of Knockespoch	Mrs S. Roberts	Mr, Mrs & Miss Bateman	4
	Footloose Freddy	Dog	4.6.81	Maurbry Marzipan	Maurbry Bethany	Miss G. Burrell	Mrs S. Thorpe	4
	Coatham Hermes	Bitch	1.8.82	Ch. Whaplode Unique	Coatham Ides of March	Mr and Mrs Gwilliam	as breeders	5
	Swindridge Mathew	Dog	1.4.82	Ch. Swindridge Ferdinand	Swindridge Geraldine	Mr and Mrs M. Wensley	as breeders	
	Finetime Sardonyx	Dog	11.11.83	Whaplode My Major	Fastacre Spartan Diamond	Mr and Mrs Findlay	Miss Thomas & Mr Churchill	4
1986	Maurbry Maisy Maiden	Bitch	25.3.81	Ch. Whaplode Unique	Maurbry My Maiden	Mrs M. Chapman	Mrs A. L. Barnes	3
	Pankraz von den drei Helman of Bernmont	Dog	8.10.82	Casar Vom Holdersberg	Herma v.d.d. Helman	Mahrlein & Schreiber	Miss P. Muggleton	3
	Bernadino Winterberg	Dog	21.10.83	Ch. Topvalley Wogans Winner	Ravensbank Katy Cube of Bernadino	Mr and Mrs Lux	as breeders	5
	Hartleapwell Secret Love	Bitch	6.1.84	Ch. Maurbry Message	Ch. Morning Star of Hartleapwell	Mrs. J. Evans	as breeder	8
	Coatham Gin N Tonic	Bitch	1.2.83	Coatham Rum N Black	Ch. Be Elect of Burtonswood	Mr and Mrs Gwilliam	Mr and Mrs D. Owen	3
	Marlender Moonraker	Dog	11.12.79	Ch. Lindenhall Capability Brown	Kempshott Tia Maria	Mr and Mrs R. Martin	as breeders	3
	Hartleapwell Magic Moments	Bitch	6.1.84	Ch. Maurbry Message	Ch. Morning Star of Hartleapwell	Mrs J. Evans	as breeder	5
	Middlepark Grand Monarque	Dog	16.12.83	Middlepark Dark Knight	Middlepark Bridgitte	Mrs S. Boulden	as breeder	4
	Woodruff Felicity	Bitch	12.7.82	Ch. Topvalley Karl	Woodruff Bush Baby	Mr and Mrs Harrison	B. Markham	5
	Bernadino Fedor	Dog	21.10.83	Ch. Topvalley Wogans Winner	Ravensbank Katy Cube of Bernadino	Mr and Mrs Lux	as breeders	3
	Finetime the Great Bear	Dog	17.4.84	Arambaskh Statesman	Pilgrimwood Gorgeous Girl	Mr and Mrs Findlay	Miss Thomas & Mr Churchill	4
	Treeburn Challenger	Dog	26.10.84	Ch. Laird O Glayva of Treeburn	Penvalla of Treeburn	Mr and Mrs R. Gardner	as breeders	3

Appendix 2: Family Trees of Noted Champions

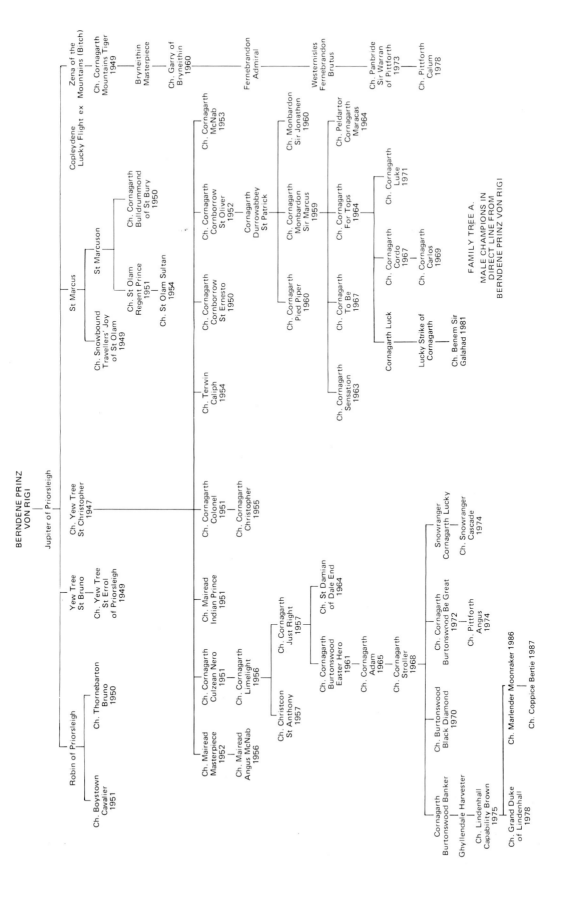

BERNDENE PRINZ
VON RIGI

Jupiter of Priorsleigh

FAMILY TREE A.

MALE CHAMPIONS IN
DIRECT LINE FROM
BERNDENE PRINZ VON RIGI

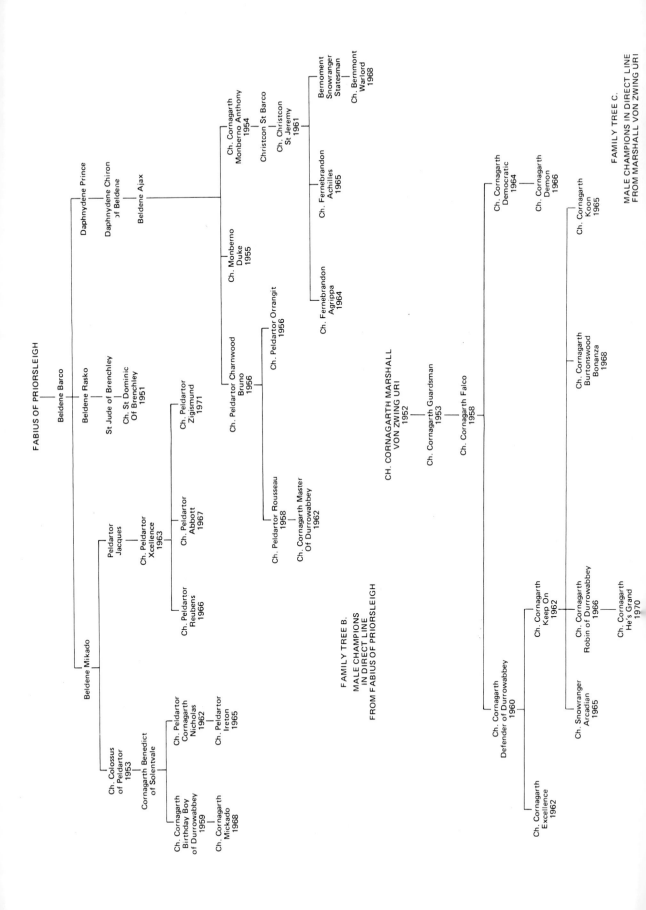

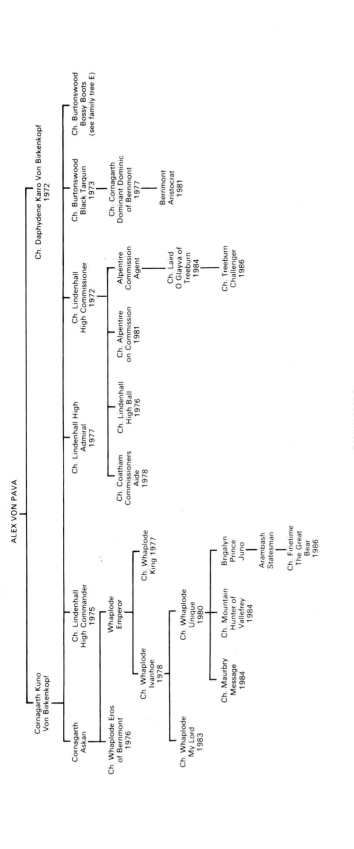

FAMILY TREE D.

MALE CHAMPIONS IN DIRECT LINE FROM ALEX VON PAVA

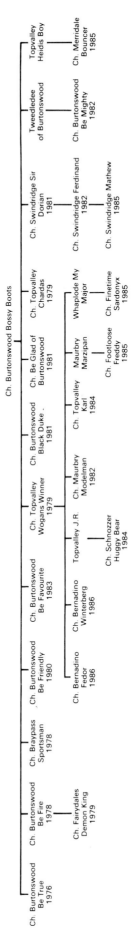

FAMILY TREE E.

DIRECT LINE FROM CH. BURTONSWOOD BOSSY BOOTS

Appendix 3: Pedigrees of Noted Champions

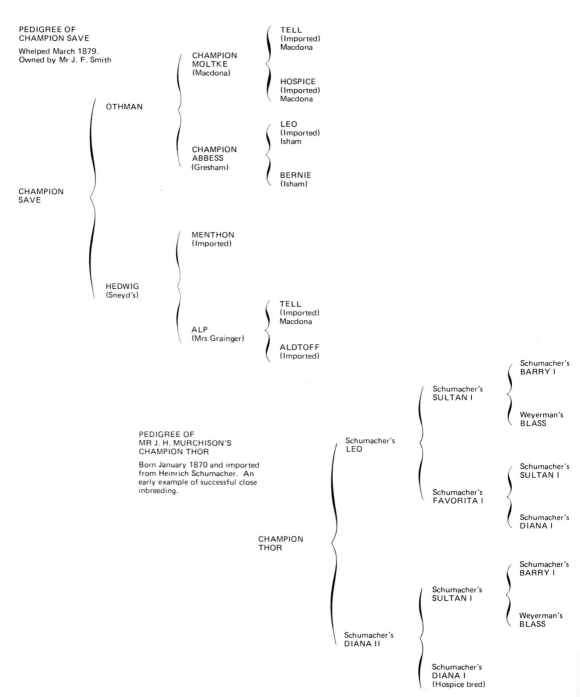

PEDIGREE OF
CHAMPION SAVE

Whelped March 1879.
Owned by Mr J. F. Smith

CHAMPION
SAVE

OTHMAN

CHAMPION
MOLTKE
(Macdona)

TELL
(Imported)
Macdona

HOSPICE
(Imported)
Macdona

CHAMPION
ABBESS
(Gresham)

LEO
(Imported)
Isham

BERNIE
(Isham)

HEDWIG
(Sneyd's)

MENTHON
(Imported)

ALP
(Mrs Grainger)

TELL
(Imported)
Macdona

ALDTOFF
(Imported)

PEDIGREE OF
MR J. H. MURCHISON'S
CHAMPION THOR

Born January 1870 and imported
from Heinrich Schumacher. An
early example of successful close
inbreeding.

CHAMPION
THOR

Schumacher's
LEO

Schumacher's
SULTAN I

Schumacher's
BARRY I

Weyerman's
BLASS

Schumacher's
FAVORITA I

Schumacher's
SULTAN I

Schumacher's
DIANA I

Schumacher's
DIANA II

Schumacher's
SULTAN I

Schumacher's
BARRY I

Weyerman's
BLASS

Schumacher's
DIANA I
(Hospice bred)

PEDIGREE OF CH. YEW TREE ST CHRISTOPHER

Born 14 September 1943.
Bred by Mrs C. E. Walker.
Owned by A. K. Gaunt.

YEW TREE ST BRUNO	JUPITER OF PRIORSLEIGH	BERNDENE PRINZ VON RIGI	FAUST VON RIGI	BARRY VON RIGI
				CH. ALMA VON RIGI
			INT. CH. HORSA VON NEUHOF	CEASAR VON RIGI
				CH. NORMA DEPPELLOR
		MONTE ROSA	ST SILVERIAS PEARL	CH. JEROME PEARL
				ST PAMELA PEARL
			CRESSWELL DUCHESS	MOORGATE MASTERPIECE
				STELLA OF MOORGARTH
	BOWMAC FRANCES	FABIUS OF PRIORSLEIGH	THE ALPINE COLOSSUS	MOORGATE MASTERPIECE
				VAGABOND QUEEN
			MONTE ROSA	ST SILVERIAS PEARL
				CRESSWELL DUCHESS
		LADY PENELOPE	CH. BERNDEAN INVADER	CH. BELDENE BRUNO
				CH. BERNDENE AILSA
			MONTEENIS MAID	ST SYLESTER PEARL
				COPLEYDENE EMPRESS
YEW TREE ST FILUMENA	CH. BERNDEAN INVADER	CH. BELDENE BRUNO	DUKE OF HOLLANDS	CH. TRIESMAGESTIS
				SILVERENE-PEARL
			PRIDE OF THE HEIGHTS	BRENIN PEARL
				QUEEN OF THE SEAS
		CH. BERNDENE AILSA	MOORGATE MASTERPIECE	CH. ST RAYMOND PEARL
				MOORGATE VIOLET
			EMIRA FLORA	INT. CH. EMIR VON JURA
				GERDA
	DINAH OF NEWBRIDGE	CH. THE MARQUIS OF WETTERHORN	MOORGATE MASTERPIECE	CH. ST RAYMOND PEARL
				MOORGATE VIOLET
			EMIRA FLORA	INT. CH. EMIR VON JURA
				GERDA
		COPLEYDENE ST MORAG	BILLIE OF RIBBESFORD	CH. MILORD BARRI-MAWR
				THE MOUNTAIN GIRL
			FELICITY	MONASTERY GUARD
				MONASTERY DUCHESS

PEDIGREE OF CH. CORNAGARTH STROLLER

Born 27 October 1966.
Owned and bred by A. K. Gaunt

CH. CORNAGARTH ADAM

- CH. CORNAGARTH BURTONSWOOD EASTER HERO
  - CH. CORNAGARTH JUST RIGHT
    - CH. CORNAGARTH LIMELIGHT
      - CH. CORNAGARTH CULZEAN NERO
      - CORNAGARTH MY OWN
    - CORNAGARTH NETTA
      - CH. CORNAGARTH GUARDSMAN
      - CH. CORNAGARTH CRYSELLA
  - CH. PRIMA DONNA OF BURTONSWOOD
    - CH. PELDARTOR CHARNWOOD BRUNO
      - BELDENE AJAX
      - MONBERNO BELLE
    - CORNAGARTH CORONET
      - CH. CORNAGARTH CULZEAN NERO
      - THORNEBARTON CELIA
- CHRISTCON ST NADIA
  - CH. CHRISTCON ST JEREMY
    - CHRISTCON ST BARCO
      - CH. CORNAGARTH MONBERNO ANTHONY
      - CORNAGARTH COMET
    - ST COLLIERS GENEVIEVE
      - BELDENE BARON
      - BUNTY THE JOYFUL
  - CHRISTCON ST BRENDA
    - CH. CORNAGARTH MONBERNO ANTHONY
      - BELDENE AJAX
      - MONBERNO BELLE
    - CORNAGARTH COMET
      - CH. YEW TREE ST CHRISTOPHER
      - YEW TREE ST KAYE

CH. CORNAGARTH BURTONSWOOD PRINCESS

- CH. CORNAGARTH FOR TOPS
  - CH. CORNAGARTH MONBARDON SIR MARCUS
    - CORNAGARTH DURROWABBEY ST PATRICK
      - CH. CORNAGARTH CORNBORROW ST OLIVER
      - CH. CORNAGARTH THORNEBARTON JUNGFRAU
    - CORNAGARTH HORSA
      - CH. CORNAGARTH GUARDSMAN
      - CH. CORNAGARTH CRYSELLA
  - CORNAGARTH KEEP ME
    - CH. CORNAGARTH DEFENDER OF DURROWABBEY
      - CH. CORNAGARTH FALCO
      - CH. CORNAGARTH DURROWABBEY ST MARIA
    - CH. PRIMA DONNA OF BURTONSWOOD
      - CH. PELDARTOR CHARNWOOD BRUNO
      - CORNAGARTH CORONET
- CH. CORNAGARTH TRUE LOVE
  - CH. CORNAGARTH MASTER OF DURROWABBEY
    - CH. PELDARTOR ROSSEAU
      - CH. PELDARTOR CHARNWOOD BRUNO
      - CH. PELDARTOR ANKA V. D. SCHLENSE
    - CH. CORNAGARTH DURROWABBEY ST MARIA
      - CH. CORNAGARTH CORNBORROW ST OLIVER
      - CH. CORNAGARTH THORNEBARTON JUNGFRAU
  - CH. CORNAGARTH MOIRA
    - CORNAGARTH MONBARDON SIR MARCUS
      - CORNAGARTH DURROWABBEY ST PATRICK
      - CORNAGARTH HORSA
    - PELDARTOR WYDELLO
      - CH. PELDARTOR ROSSEAU
      - CH. PELDARTOR LUCIA

PEDIGREE OF INT. CH.
BURTONSWOOD BOSSY BOOTS

Born 10 July 1971.
Owned and bred by Miss M. Hindes

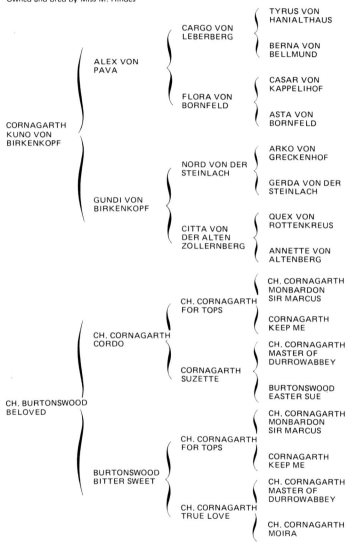

Appendix 4: Numbers of Registrations with the Kennel Club

1947	247	1957	155	1967	292	1977*	191
1948	304	1958	165	1968	322	1978	517*
1949	325	1959	232	1969	288	1979	988
1950	241	1960	192	1970	376	1980	713
1951	255	1961	235	1971	342	1981	559
1952	192	1962	259	1972	498	1982	626
1953	231	1963	267	1973	604	1983	515
1954	251	1964	195	1974	592	1984	513
1955	248	1965	328	1975	389	1985	516
1956	184	1966	217	1976*	222	1986	486

Figures for 1976/77/78 relate to Active registrations only, a special scheme being in operation for these three years.

Bibliography

W. F. Barazetti. *The St Bernard Book* (1955)

W. Bullen and Nora Dicken. *The St Bernard and English Mastiff* (1936)

Hugh Dalziel. *The St Bernard – its History, Points, Breeding and Rearing* (1886)

M. Denlinger. *The Complete St Bernard* (1952)

J. Fleischli. *The St Bernard* (1954)

Frederick Gresham. *The St Bernard* (in *The New Book of the Dog*) (1907)

F.D. Grey. *The Dogs of St Bernard* (1903)

Ferelith Hamilton (ed). *The World Encyclopaedia of Dogs* (1971)

Clifford Hubbard. *Dogs in Britain* (1948)

Hutchinson's Dog Encyclopaedia (1935)

Percy Manning. *The St Bernard* (in *Kennel Encyclopaedia*) (1910)

Chanoine Marquis. *Les Chiens du Grande St Bernard* (1973)

And other general literature on dogs.

Index